Geography and Younger Children

Geography and Younger Children

An outline of theory and practice

Eric J. Barker

 University of London Press Ltd

ISBN 0 340 15991 X Boards
ISBN 0 340 15992 8 Unibook
Copyright © 1974 Eric J. Barker

University of London Press Ltd,
St Paul's House, Warwick Lane, London EC4P 4AH

Printed and bound in Great Britain by
Hazell Watson & Viney Ltd,
Aylesbury, Bucks

19445

Contents

Eric J. Barker died at the early age of 47, only a short while after he had completed this book, and it is in a sense a memorial to him. He would have asked for nothing better: from boyhood and throughout his career as a geographer and a teacher he was intensely interested in the earth and its peoples; the different landscapes and ways of life. These all caught his vital imagination and insatiable curiosity and it is this which he was so happy to share with the hundreds of young people who may benefit from this book.

The publishers are grateful to the following for permission to reproduce maps and photographs: Aerofilms (71); Keystone Press (10); Ordnance Survey (45).

Part 1

Geography with younger children

I

An evolving pattern

'—Tyne, Wear, Tees, 'umber—' muttered Art Kipps, struggling to recall what he had learnt at school. He failed, but H. G. Wells, his creator, was more successful in reminding us of the way in which geography was frequently presented in the last century. Often it was little more than such arid little lists.

In several ways such geography teaching presented the teacher with far fewer problems than it does now: the subject had simply defined aims and well-known and well-trusted methods of achieving these aims. School geography in modern Britain originated in the 'dissenting academies' on the eve of the nineteenth century: certainly it was being taught in these schools at a time when it was absent from the timetables of the great public schools. Much of this geography was fundamentally economic geography. That this was so is understandable. Many of the pupils were the sons of businessmen and factory owners: the social products of the Industrial Revolution. For such children, destined to enter family firms, such studies were almost an aspect of vocational training. For a son to learn the names of the chief cotton growing countries made sense to a man who could quote precise prices on the Manchester Exchange. He paid his son's fees and felt that he was getting value for money. The teacher, for his part, gave instruction along the lines that he was required to follow. His task might be dull but it was at least clear-cut.

The 'capes and bays' geography—the rote learning of lists that spread rapidly with the coming of state education—could also be justified in terms of the conditions of the time. The increasing complexity of industrial organisation made necessary a work force that could read, write neatly, calculate accurately, and which had some store of general knowledge. Much of the geography that was taught fell under this last heading. This geography was fundamentally a listing of information rather than a discipline involving reasoning. A pupil was expected to know that Paris was the capital of France—but the question why Paris held this dominant position was seldom asked by either pupil or teacher.

It is easy, with the advantage of hindsight, to be a little contemptuous of this teaching. Yet even in the 'capes and bays' period, teachers were searching, as we are today, for techniques that would make the learning process more efficient. Lists were given an interest, and set in doggerel verse:

Now Jolly Tars are preparing the ship,
We round these islands will take a trip

Mnemonics were used, and rhyme and even singing, as in:

G is for Goshen, a rich and good land,
H is for Horeb where Moses did stand

Although a text book from this period will often amuse a modern teacher, many teachers will envy the simplicity of the task that their predecessors faced. It is not difficult to make children memorise lists providing that society permits—or indeed expects and requires—a rigid discipline in the classroom. In addition to this results were easily and satisfactorily measurable. It is far easier to test a child's ability to recite a list of the rivers of England than it is to measure a child's ability to reason along geographical lines.

Other themes were added. Thus the half century before the outbreak of the First World War was marked by the rise of clearly defined patriotism. A world political map became one of the standard pieces of equipment: indeed it was often the only map provided. Empire Day became a major event in schools and it remained so well into the '30s. Often the morning of Empire Day was devoted entirely to lessons on various aspects of Britain and the Empire: a morning which culminated in a ceremony in the playground during which the flag was raised on the school flagpole. The afternoon was usually a half holiday to impress the importance of it all on the children. This interest in Britain's imperial role was reflected in school geography. It is interesting that something of this still lingers. An analysis of school text books still reveals a disproportionate amount of space devoted to former British territories.

However the rise of the imperial theme did not add greatly to the problems of the teacher. Work on the areas within the Empire was almost entirely descriptive. Moreover these descriptions were given to children who were without the sometimes disconcertingly up-to-date material provided by television: material which, as modern teachers know to their cost, often shows up school text books as out of date and inaccurate.

Slowly the pattern changed. By the period between the wars geography courses had become more ambitious in their scope and contained far more geographical reasoning and far more weighting on the full understanding of geographical ideas. *Geography First Series*, by Archer and Thomas, first published in the '30s by Ginn, was an outstanding junior school text book series of the time. In the fourth book of this series the authors took the surprisingly modern theme of the world's population and examined and compared conditions in the crowded lands and the empty lands. This marked a real advance on anything that had gone before.

During this period the study of geography was developing rapidly in the universities and slowly this development affected schools. Some difficulties were however encountered: the case of the Eskimoes providing one example. Academic geographers became interested in these people because Eskimoes offer a very clear cut case of a culture that was unable to develop further because of the harshness of the environment. Eskimo culture, as it was before it was affected by outside influence, was an object of serious study. However in schools this original culture was presented as though it was still in being. Children in junior schools often gained an astonishingly detailed knowledge of igloos, kayaks, umiaks and the rest. Indeed many children left school knowing more about Eskimoes than they did about the whole of China.

These changes had the result of making the teacher's task more difficult. Teaching a pupil to think logically and clearly involves very special skills. There was the additional difficulty that it was at this time that emphasis began to be placed on the importance of children finding out for themselves. This new attitude was brought out succinctly by the 1931 Report on the Primary School by the Consultative Committee under the chairmanship of Hadow. This report contained the statement: 'The curriculum is to be thought of in terms of activity and experience rather than knowledge to be acquired and facts to be stored.'

However a teacher at this time, when preparing a scheme of work, had at least one problem solved automatically. Geography was, almost invariably, marked as such on the timetable. In thousands of junior classes the time allotted to this was fixed. Usually two periods a week were set aside for this subject, so it was relatively easy to estimate how much could be covered in a term or in a year. Anyway the text book for the year gave a guide as to a reasonable number of themes to be covered.

It is rare to find a primary school that still follows a rigid time-table, an inflexible syllabus, and a fixed pattern of formal lessons. The whole situation has been evolving in the light of recent discoveries concerning the way in which children learn and the way in which they develop.

The degree of change that schools have undergone varies widely. If one visits a large number of schools a very wide range of opinion is obvious, with some schools putting far more emphasis on the timetable and syllabus than others. Many factors are involved: changes in schools have been seriously hampered by overcrowded and out-dated buildings and by inadequate allowances for books and materials. The nature of the area in which the school stands is also important. Among some of the strongest supporters of a clearly defined syllabus are those head teachers whose schools are in areas where frequent staff changes have taken place. Such teachers claim that a high degree of direction, though professionally undesirable, is a small price to pay for continuity. Certainly it avoids the situation whereby children study 'communications' as a topic every year for four

The author's father with his class in 1905. The disciplined formality of the whole scene and the lack of 'class-room clutter' contrasts sharply with modern schools. It is worth noting that this photograph was taken in a prosperous south coast town which enjoyed a reputation as a progressive area: there is no question here of underprivileged or deprived children.

years: a situation that has arisen in schools where a succession of young teachers have, in desperation it would seem, seized on a theme that is exceptionally well documented.

But such situations only apply to a minority of schools. Generally the pattern of teaching has changed to a marked degree. Indeed the phrase 'classroom revolution' has even been coined to describe this change. A visitor to a typical primary school class—particularly one of the younger classes—is likely to find that the children are engaged in a wide variety of activities, some studying books, some writing busily, some painting, drawing or making models, and some, quite possibly, carrying out experiments with improvised apparatus in a corner. It is far from easy to visit such a class and say 'this is geography' or 'this is English'. The familiar subject labels do not apply—or rather they do not apply in the traditional way.

Such a seemingly confused classroom situation is very common where teachers have decided to apply 'topic', 'project', 'centre of interest', or 'integrated day' methods. All these terms are used: each has a slightly different shade of meaning, but each presents a similar classroom situation to a casual visitor and each presents similar difficulties to the teacher.

Control is clearly one basic problem: it calls for considerable professional skills and meticulous planning if the large number of children in the classroom are to be kept gainfully occupied all the time. The second basic problem lies in planning. A paradox of these recently developed teaching methods is that though the children may not meet geography as a formal academic subject in at least the first few years of their primary education, they may well complete this part of their school life knowing a great deal of geography. Exactly the same may be said of history, science and other traditional school subjects. The teacher has the responsibility of guiding children so that they meet these ideas in the course of their work. Clearly this is far more demanding of professional skills than giving a pattern of more formal lessons based on a fixed syllabus.

A specific example may serve to illustrate this point. In the kind of classroom situation just described, if the visitor asks a child what is at hand, the answer may well be something along the lines of 'We're making a "keeping warm" book.' In a 'topic' approach the children study some central theme that is truly topical: some theme related to the children and which impinges on their interests. On a cold February day, when the class has been interrupted by the caretaker struggling to keep the radiators hot, 'How we keep warm' might well prove a suitable theme. Perhaps this work begins with a class discussion in which the children help the teacher to build up a blackboard summary of work that can be done under this heading. Such a period, incidentally, may well ressemble a fixed formal lesson in that the children are seated and working in unison with the teacher. It differs from such a lesson largely in the attitude of the teacher. Attempts will be made to draw information from the class: attempts made to help the children to arrange ideas logically, rather than to give factual instruction. Obviously where facts are needed the teacher will supply them—but this is an incidental rather than a central feature of the lesson. It is indicative of this attitude that some teachers of younger children refer to such periods as 'class meetings' rather than lessons. This spread of educational jargon may perhaps be deplored but the attitude that it implies is interesting.

But whatever terms are used, the period ends with a list of lines of enquiry. Thus under 'How we keep warm' the list may include:

> fuels that we use: coal, electricity, gas, oil;
> how radiators work;
> how we heat our homes;
> the clothes we wear in winter;
> what our clothes are made of;
> how people keep warm in other lands;
> how people have kept warm in the past.

Some of these lines of enquiry have little bearing on geography. 'How people kept warm in the past' is obviously an historical theme. However there is a great deal here that is directly concerned with geography, and these elements can be used by a teacher to introduce geographical ideas. If the school heating system burns fuel oil, the questions 'What is fuel oil?', 'Where does it come from?', 'How does it reach us?' arise naturally and logically. A teacher may decide to guide a group of children towards an attempt to answer these questions. The methods by which this work can be done are discussed elsewhere in this book, but the group might eventually produce little folders containing information based on a list of some of the men who must work in order for the school radiators to give any heat at all. The list might include a worker at an oil well, a man who maintains an oil pipe line, a seaman on a tanker, a dock worker, the driver of a road tanker, etc. What can be brought out by the teacher is a fundamental point of geography: that nearly everything that we use depends not on a single workman's efforts but on the efforts of a chain of interdependent workers. It is stressed that this is the basic idea. It is brought out here by talking of fuel oil but it could equally well have been brought out by finding out about the people who must work in order for the children to eat bread —the farmer in Canada, the seaman on the North Atlantic, the mill worker at the dockside, etc.—would have served just as well. Whether a child should know more about the production of oil than the production of wheat or vice versa is perhaps of academic interest: certainly it would be hoped that by the time a child reached the secondary stage he knew a little about both—but this is not the point at issue here.

Implicit in all this is the idea that a teacher must know exactly what geographical ideas a child should meet during the early stages of education and that teachers should be able to judge when individuals have reached the stage when these ideas can be usefully introduced. There is little that is controversial about this statement: clearly a teacher should have a goal: clearly teaching should be purposeful. Indeed it is over this point that teaching can be sharply divided from baby-minding. Equally to try to introduce too difficult an idea to too young a child is absurd. However, putting this into practice is less simple. There is no agreed list of geographical ideas that children should have met by any given age: nothing that a teacher can use as an agreed syllabus in religious education can be used. This is a matter that is discussed more fully elsewhere in this book, but it can be remarked here that even were such a list to be compiled it would only have value for a given moment of time. Two examples may be given to illustrate the point. Recently a St Albans primary school took a football team to play an away match. The team travelled by rail—and it was found that three of the team had never been on a train before in their lives. All their previous experience of travel had been by car, by coach, or even by air. The closure of lines and the increase of car ownership coupled with the rising cost of rail travel have given a pattern that is very different from that which existed little more than a decade ago. Evidently it is no longer possible to talk of rail travel to children and expect them to have experience of this: that is, in this respect, the situation has changed.

A second example can be taken from the idea that the earth is a sphere. This may well be considered a difficult idea for young children: their ideas of spatial relationships and distance are different from those of an adult. On the other hand it is important to remember that Yuri Gagarin made his journey in space in 1961. Children whose whole lives have been spent in the era of space travel have much less difficulty in grasping the idea of a spherical earth than the children of earlier periods. Many elements of the child's environment have helped here: the impact of television, of books and stories, and even of children's comics. All have contributed to the ease with which children understand the basic idea. A child today is much more likely to think in terms of a spherical earth than is a member of a generation brought up to think in terms of a flat map. Indeed it is not unknown for an able eleven-year old, asked to point in the direction of, say, China, to point downwards in an easterly direction rather than towards the east as many adults will do.

There was a time when there was a clear distinction between school work and play. The dividing line has become more and more blurred with the realisation that when interests are awakened learning takes place more rapidly: that the enthusiasms of play can be used in school. Indeed the phrase 'play-way' was coined

The idea of the earth as a sphere in space has been brought home to children by television, by features in children's comics and, as here, by space flight. This photograph of the earth was taken by Apollo 8 astronauts as they came from behind the moon.

to describe such methods. Where such techniques are used yet further responsibility is thrust upon teachers: the need to devise and select activities that children will enjoy but which nevertheless have a sound educational justification. This qualification is important: it marks the difference between the work of an educator and the efforts of a neighbour keeping children out of harm's way during a mother's brief absence.

The ways in which the play element is often used in primary schools have led to many misunderstandings between parents and schools and even between managers and staffs. Ambitious parents may be forgiven for misunderstanding what has taken place when a child, questioned about the day's work, talks of painting a picture, making models out of scrap materials or taking part in improvised dramatic activity. Thus an additional problem that teachers must face is that the public is sometimes deeply suspicious of what is being done.

Meanwhile the development of educational ideas is tending to widen the gap rather than close it. Thus a comparatively recent extension of the play element is in geographical games. These are described in more detail elsewhere in this book, but it can be stressed here that many of these games are true games in the sense that *Ludo* or *Monopoly* are games. The value of such games lies in the fact that while children are playing they are at the same time gaining an appreciation of geographical ideas.

It is the particular skill of a good teacher of younger children to know how to use this play element and gain the maximum value from it. Yet devising such activities and using them fully is far from easy. A teacher may well envy his predecessor's clear-cut list of the rivers of England.

2

Aims in the teaching of geography

Just as strategy differs from tactics, so long term aims differ from immediate objectives. Those concerned with the education of young children are faced with the problems of both. Since the nature of the immediate objective of a lesson, or indeed a group of lessons, is subject to long term considerations it is desirable to establish these first in any planning.

Planning is, of course, not restricted to those lessons when geography is to be taught, for any aspect of the curriculum involves similar basic problems. Here, however, the particular concern is geography and geography lessons. Clearly the validity of any arguments that are advanced here depends on the assumption that geography is to be taught at all. It has already been pointed out in the previous chapter that some schools merge geography with other branches of study to the point where the subject cannot be distinguished easily by a visitor to the classroom. This is an aspect that requires closer examination at this point. The Plowden Report[1] includes the clear and unequivocal statement that 'most junior schools allocate specific weekly periods to geography'. Given this, a consideration of the difficulties of planning geography lessons needs no justification. However the Plowden Report was published in 1967 and much of the information that it gives was, of necessity, garnered over several earlier years. Since this information was gathered together the rate of change in junior schools as a whole has certainly not lessened: indeed more schools appear ready to experiment than

1. *Children and their Primary Schools.* A Report of the Central Advisory Council for Education (England).

ever before. These experimental changes include moves towards an undifferentiated timetable and towards classroom practices in which various forms of study are compounded and where the children follow 'topic', 'centre of interest' or 'project' approaches. Under such forms of organisation the subject 'geography' may well not appear on the timetable. This, of course, is already the case in infant schools where the formal division of knowledge into such subjects as geography has not been applied for many years.

Some figures are available here. Recently H.M. Inspectors carried out a survey of 215 primary schools widely distributed over England. A summary of this survey was published in 1972 (J. W. Morris, in *Trends in Education*, Oct. 1972). This stated that 19 per cent of the schools involved in the sample retained geography as a separate subject. In a further 20 per cent geographical material kept a separate identity although it was presented in some form of integrated study. In 61 per cent of the schools geography was absorbed in combined studies: studies which appeared under various names such as social studies and environmental studies.

Nevertheless, although the word 'geography' may not be used in a number of schools, this is certainly not to say that geography and geographical ideas are not taught. It is helpful to make the analogy with economics. Here is a branch of learning that is never named as such on the timetable of any school for younger children. Yet this is not to say that economic ideas are never taught: indeed quite the opposite is the case. A class of eleven-year olds, about to leave the primary stage, will usually be able to explain many ideas that belong to economics: the meaning of 'profit' and 'loss', what is meant by 'wholesale' as applied to the purchase of goods, and what is implied by the words 'import' and 'export'. In precisely the same way it would be expected that such a class—even if the school was deliberately avoiding a subject-based approach—would not only be able to give such facts as that Paris is the capital of France but would also be able to make an attempt at the far more difficult task of explaining what a 'capital city' means.

Thus, irrespective of the approach followed by a school, geographical facts and geographical ideas are presented to children. (In justice to the advocates of integration it must be said that it is no part of their philosophy that this should not be so.) If such ideas are to be taught it would seem essential that careful planning should accompany such teaching.

Geography embodies a huge corpus of material. If only because there is a limited amount of time available, and leaving out considerations of suitability for the moment, a selection must be made. Making such a selection is one of the most difficult problems facing a teacher, for, as was emphasised earlier, it is impossible to draw up a definitive list graded to the needs of differing age/ability groups spread over a wide area. Attempts have been made to do this—chiefly in the U.S.A.—but none have been satisfactory since children vary so widely. The background experience of children in a Somerset village is so different from that of children in a Liverpool suburb that comparison becomes impossible. Further the material that is presented to children changes rapidly. Thus when Sir Francis Chichester made his single-handed voyage round the world many teachers followed his adventure with their classes: the material presented to those children differed from that presented to their predecessors and from that presented in schools at the moment. It can be regretted but it must be admitted that it is impossible to draw up any system of 'geographical ages' similar to the familiar 'reading ages', nor can there be an 'agreed syllabus' for geography as is the case in religious education.

It is tempting to tackle the problem by examining existing school schemes and seeing what is being done at present, thus basing long-term planning on the experience of practising teachers. One initial difficulty here is that many schools do not use a clear-cut scheme of work. This statement can be backed by figures given in a 1972 survey by H.M. Inspectorate, which pointed out that 43 per cent of the schools visited did not have formal schemes although some of these schools relied on a current television series to provide a framework and so, presumably, the programme details can be accepted as a scheme of sorts. However where written schemes or even verbal accounts are available it is worth noting that what is given may be misleading. To take a single specific example, many children still study 'cocoa' as a topic during the second year of the junior stage. Whether 'cocoa' is a wise choice or not is a point that need not concern us immediately. It is, however, worth examining this topic in order to analyse the problems faced by a teacher in such a seemingly simple matter. The first question that might be asked concerns what the children actually learn during a series of lessons on this topic. An immediate and somewhat facile answer to this is that they will learn that cocoa is made from the beans produced by a tree that grows in Ghana. Obviously this is true: the children will indeed learn this. However it prompts a second series of questions: is this something that the children need to know? Is there any special merit in knowing these facts? Is there any good reason why children should know about cocoa rather than about asbestos (to cite a second African product but one that appears very much more rarely on school syllabuses). It is perhaps not easy to justify time spent by children learning about cocoa except perhaps in terms of general knowledge. Nor is it entirely convincing to argue that this is a topic in which children are especially interested. When a child asks 'How is chocolate made?' the question is frequently less an expression of interest in economic geography than an idea that could be rephrased 'Is chocolate hard to make and could we make some here to eat now?' Besides, returning to the example given earlier, a picture of men clad in asbestos fire-fighting clothing is just as likely to create an interest in the minds of junior school boys at least as is the idea of a cup of cocoa.

This argument appears completely destructive. However it should not be interpreted as implying that 'cocoa' is an unsuitable theme in a scheme of work. What is stressed is that the theme is no more than a vehicle for those ideas that the teacher may decide are suited to the needs of the children. Thus it can be brought home that the reason why the difficult and expensive business of transporting cocoa beans from Ghana is undertaken at all is because these beans cannot be grown here. This may lead, under the guidance of the teacher, to the class finding out what other things cannot be grown here. How then, the children may be challenged, did people in this country manage before there were fast and reliable ships? The children encounter the quite startling idea that—with the exception of milk and water—virtually everything that they drink—tea, coffee, cocoa, lemonade, orange squash, Coca-cola, and so on—were unknown a relatively short time ago, historically speaking. All this work thus reinforces the geographical concept of differing environments: this is the basic idea underlying this treatment of the topic.

Many alternative interpretations of the topic can be employed. For example weight might be placed on the idea that none of us can enjoy a simple bar of chocolate without relying on the efforts of a whole chain of men and women many of whom live at a great distance from us. Here stress is laid on a difficult idea: a foundation is laid for the recognition of the inter-dependence of all mankind. Alternatively a teacher might well decide to use the topic to give practice in mapping skills. The children might study pictures of a cocoa plantation and use the information thus gained to build up a simple map. They might learn about the voyage from Takoradi and try to follow this on a globe or on a map. Under these conditions it is the skill of mapping that is receiving attention.

A further complication is that since these various interpretations are not mutually exclusive, some teachers might employ them all during the work on the single topic.

Clearly the listing of such a theme as 'cocoa' on a syllabus does not really solve the problems of planning. It is still necessary for a teacher to decide what is of value and how it should be introduced at a particular point of time with a particular class. Perhaps the nearest approach to a check-list is achieved by applying certain tests to the material that is to be taught. Thus it can be asked whether the material to be taught comes under the heading of general knowledge: knowledge that is defined here as information that well-informed children might reasonably be expected to possess. In the case of cocoa, the knowledge of the existence and position of Ghana is an example of information that falls into this category. There is a risk here, however, that we fall into a circular argument: that most people learned about cocoa when at school, so most people know about cocoa, therefore knowledge about cocoa growing is general knowledge that can reasonably be taught in school. Set out thus baldly the fallacy is obvious, but it is precisely this fallacy that keeps igloo building a staple in junior school syllabuses.

Despite this, the test of whether what is being taught is truly general knowledge forms a useful sieve that helps obviate unnecessary detail. For example a teachers' manual for an existing series of junior school books gives the following information:

'The tree which produces cocoa is native to Central and South America, but is widely grown in the African tropics. The tree, which will thrive only on moist lowland areas, stands some 20 ft. high. The leaves are dark green and oval. Small red star-shaped flowers form on the main stem. Subsequently pods form as shown.'

It is not unreasonable to ask how much of this is really general knowledge, and if this is indeed general knowledge why it was thought necessary to include it in a manual for teachers. It must be allowed, in fairness to the book, that some of this detail is needed if the children are to form clear mental images. Thus the fact that the trees are comparable to apple trees in height, and not to pine trees or gooseberry bushes, is helpful, even though few people would expect children to give an accurate figure if asked to estimate the height of a cocoa tree. The point that is stressed here is that there is sometimes a danger that an inexperienced teacher, once embarked on well-prepared subject matter, may teach as though the objective was to give every child an encyclopedic knowledge of the topic.

A second criterion that can be applied in testing the value of material is to ask if it helps children to achieve a useful skill. It was suggested earlier that some, at least, of the work that could be centred about the topic of 'cocoa' could be map work. Here at least is something that classifies as a useful skill. An ability to read a map is valuable in both work and leisure: it is clearly less valuable by far than being able to read a book, but it might well be compared with the ability to read music.

Value can also be claimed for those aspects of geography which help children to see relationships and which help children to develop logical thought. This statement sounds forbidding in terms of young children, but these ideas may still be present. Thus if children are shown pictures of houses in the cocoa growing areas of Ghana, they will learn that a familiar and traditional pattern of house is of a bungalow type with the rooms set round a courtyard, and that often part of this courtyard is shielded by a verandah. Many of the domestic chores are carried out under this verandah. Now there is a clear link between this and climatic conditions: a link that a skilled teacher will establish very quickly with a few questions. In this, one aspect of the relationship that exists between man and his environment is demonstrated. In studying pictures with children and in separating houses and weather for study a teacher is helping children to take the first steps in geographical analysis: by realising that there is a link between these seemingly totally different things children are beginning to make what at a much higher level would be termed geographical synthesis.

Finally there is that value that is inherent in any material presented to younger children that is likely to awaken interests and to maintain enquiry in their minds.

The sheer complexity of geography has already been stressed, and this can be illustrated by merely glancing down the contents list of any copy of the numerous learned journals devoted to geography. Clearly the interests of geographers range from studies of the physical landscape to the application of mathematical techniques, to the understanding of the layout of cities from the physical conditions of the upper atmosphere to the political aspects of varied distributions. It is this width of interest that gives geography a special educational value. Attempts to divide the subject into, say, 'earth sciences' and 'human studies' as is done in many American schools, rob it of this value.

Yet despite this, to assess what we should expect children to achieve in geography; to set out long-term aims, it is perhaps convenient to divide geography; to separate certain aspects and to see what can be hoped for in each. Geographical terminology, themes centred in the immediate vicinity of school and home, studies of more distant places, and the skills both of mapping and of allied geographical skills may be examined.

A beginning may be made in the case of geographical terminology. A point that is often made in discussions on geography with younger children is that we would hope that children should build up a geographical vocabulary during the early years of their education. As a statement this is probably unexceptional. It does, however, lack the precision that a practising teacher will require. It is difficult, for example, to define a geographical term. Words such as 'fjord' or 'glacier' are probably sufficiently restricted in their use to be regarded as specific to the subject, but it is doubtful whether words like 'hill' or 'river' can be regarded as strictly geographical even though the study of hills and rivers is certainly the concern of geography teaching. Further, how far is it either possible or justifiable to go in the teaching of such terms? The appearance, some years ago, of a book entitled *A Dictionary of Geography* could be taken to suggest that the terminology of the subject is moving dangerously near jargon if such a glossary is required. Attempts to resolve the problem of what should be taught have been made by painstaking research: research carried on principally by the detailed analysis of the terms used in existing text books. Some of the findings of such research have been illuminating, but really such work is rather more in the nature of a record of what has been taught rather than a list of the terms that should be taught.

More important than the number and complexity of the terms to be taught, is the degree of comprehension that children have of these terms. Children who have been taught how a thermometer works and who appear to know a great deal about measuring temperatures in degrees are still frequently puzzled by such a question as 'If the thermometer shows 15°C do I need a pullover when I go out?' Similarly children who have been shown a large number of photographs of mountains may appear to understand the term 'mountain' completely. Yet these same children can be disappointed by their first sight of Cross Fell, Snowdon or Ben Nevis. For such children the flat-topped summit of Ingleborough bears little relation to a 'proper mountain' which should have a sharp snow-covered peak that is almost spike-like in form. Indeed children have been known to have been confused by the idea that Hillary and Tensing climbed Everest together: they find it difficult to appreciate that there was room on the peak for both men.

Despite these problems some indication of a long-term aim emerges. Perhaps it may be stated that children should leave the earlier stage of their education able to conjure up an accurate mental picture from any description provided that the description is sufficiently clear and provided that it does not contain terms that are so uncommon that they might be considered part of the technical vocabulary of an advanced student. One does not automatically expect an eleven-year old to know what is meant by a 'wadi'. The term may never have been used in his hearing. However one might hope that a description of a desert valley, bare of all grass and trees, with steep rocky sides and a dry floor littered with rock fragments, would be enough for the same child to form a mental image that was not too far from the truth.

Many authorities on education have stressed the importance of the immediate environment in the teaching of geography to young children. Since this topic is dealt with elsewhere in this book, the arguments need not be rehearsed here, but clearly primary school objectives will include many ideas that are locally based. What children might know was set out in some detail in an official Ministry of Education booklet, *Geography and Education*, that was published in 1961. Here it was suggested that children might know something of weather conditions and local building materials, and that children living in towns might be expected to know about such things as the main roads in and out of the town, the markets, the kinds and positions of factories, the rivers, canals, bridges, castles, old walls, railway stations—and 'something of the lives of its better known citizens'. The same account also stresses 'the importance of those immaterial things that go to make up the personality of the district', instancing, for Notting-

A child's concept of a mountain can be very inaccurate. Here Sir Edmund Hillary and Sherpa Tensing do not have room to stand side by side on the peak of Mount Everest.

ham, the significance of 'men of forest green as well as of cigar-
ettes and lace'.

This gives a clear lead. However it does hint at a somewhat
ideal if not idyllic set of cirumstances. Teachers whose schools are
set in a great stretch of virtually identical nineteenth century
terrace houses may be forgiven if they deny the relevance of this
to their circumstances.

A more recent pamphlet (*Education Pamphlet* no. 59, published
by the D.E.S. in 1972) deals with the same matter. This asks the
question as to what the primary school can expect of its leavers
as far as geography is concerned. The answer given, in so far as
the local area is concerned, is that the children 'would have
examined at first hand selected features of their own local
environment—its weather, its surface features both natural and
man-made, and something of the economic activity of its in-
habitants'. Again this gives a clear lead although it is still not easy
to apply this advice to many school areas. This is not a criticism
of the statement: rather is it an admission that because of the
wide diversity of local areas probably all that can be set out is
that a child should be helped towards an appreciation of those
geographical relationships that can be illustrated clearly and
directly from the immediate environment.

When consideration is given to more distant areas, including
both places within the child's own country and places selected
from the world as a whole, the task of setting down more precise
aims becomes even more difficult and any attempt to do this for
general application must be even more vague. One difficulty
comes in deciding upon the proportion of time that should be
allotted to the study of more distant places. Some teachers have
campaigned vigorously for very heavy weighting upon the
study of the local environment: in some cases to the exclusion of
studies of distant places except perhaps in the upper classes of the
age range that is our concern here. Others have sought a balance:
but where the balance is to be struck is very much a matter for
the judgement of the teachers concerned. Two points are however
widely agreed. First it is clearly impossible to deal with all
distant places. Thus a teacher dealing with the fuels used locally

may well be forced to decide whether to extend this to the study of coal mining areas or to the study of the natural gas areas beneath the North Sea. It is often the case that time does not allow for both. The second point of agreement is that the way in which the material is presented is of importance. The matter of the presentation of distant places is discussed more fully in chapter 11, but it may be said here that the traditional regional treatment is unsuited to the needs of young children. Instead a choice must be made from a variety of presentations. This again raises the problem of selection: which method is the most effective for a particular group of children given a particular set of circumstances?

As with matters pertaining to a geographical vocabulary, comprehension on the part of the children is a vital matter where distant places are studied. Most teachers will have heard the anecdote of the child, asked to show the entry of Christ into Jerusalem, who drew a picture showing Jesus carrying a briefcase marked with the initials 'J.C.' This does not indicate a lack of reverence, but merely a failure to recognise that what a modern parent carries to work was not a familiar object in the Palestine of the period. Exactly the same lack of understanding is shown by children in their geographical work. Coal mines are drawn in terms of the holes dug by workmen mending roads; ocean-going shipping is portrayed as though it was similar to the pleasure boats drawn up on the beach remembered from last year's holiday; trawler crews are described in terms of slipping back into harbour in time to have tea before it gets dark.

Aims, as far as distant places are concerned, can thus only be given in general terms. Perhaps all that can be said is that children should be given the opportunity to form clear impressions of parts of the world that contrast sharply with the immediate locality: that they should be helped to realise that not all mankind lives in the way that is customary in their little areas. This realisation can be linked with at least the beginnings of explanations of why places differ. With the really able children this can, perhaps, be widened (as a recent report by H.M. Inspectorate suggests) to include the realisation that populations differ in the technical and capital resources available to deal with the natural environment.

In the case of map work much more precision is possible. Very many experienced teachers have found that younger children can, given suitable guidance, develop considerable skills here. The whole topic is developed more fully in chapter 4, but clearly an aim in the teaching of geography is to give children the opportunity to develop these skills to the highest level of which they are capable.

Sir Halford Mackinder described maps as 'the tools of geography'. Even with young children the use of maps is a fundamental technique. There are also other skills that might well be considered in any attempt to assess aims. Thus young children have a quick and lively sense of curiosity. They are essentially observant. Geography teaching should aim at preserving this curiousity and indeed extending it, by showing children how what they see relates to them. Such teaching can also aim at giving precision to the observation of children by showing how the material can be recorded in ways that are meaningful to them.

Geography for younger children has thus been divided into four sections: vocabulary topics, themes centred on the area, studies of distant places, and the development of maps and allied skills. A final point arises from this division. It is that the geography presented to children, whether offered as a single subject or as a part of a combined course, can not be considered fully satisfactory unless all of these aspects are represented.

3
Planning for immediate objectives

So far planning has been considered in terms of a whole series of lessons: in terms of a year or even of a whole school course. Alternatively a different scale can be adopted and the planning of each single period can be considered. Which approach is the more helpful to a teacher probably depends on length of experience. A teacher with some length of service will have developed techniques of handling a single lesson and will be far more concerned with long term considerations: a student on teaching practice will, very naturally, be more concerned with the single lesson that lies ahead.

Whichever attitude is taken most teachers will agree that the loneliest moment in the professional career of any teacher comes early during training. This is the moment when the raw teacher is left in sole charge of a class for the first time. The majority of teachers will recall the flash of panic experienced in this situation. Certainly it is the moment that underlines very heavily the need for previous planning: the need to decide beforehand exactly how the lesson is to be conducted.

Such planning must, logically, have an objective: indeed it has already been stressed that this is where teaching differs from child minding. The point is sufficiently obvious not to be laboured here. What is not so immediately obvious is that the objective declared to the class may be very different from the true objective. When dealing with a topic taken in the manner discussed in the previous chapter, children at the age of eight will accept the setting up of an exhibition of their work as an end in itself. To them this is the objective, but the teacher will have a target that, though less obvious, has a more lasting value.

Planning a lesson clearly entails the selection of material that has geographical value and which is also suitable for the age and ability of the children. It is here that a division is often found. Children's interests are frequently captured most readily by the spectacular, the unusual, or even the bizarre. They like to hear of Maoris armed with elaborate stone axes, of head-hunting savages, or of large and dangerous wild animals. These are frequently just the very points that a teacher will not want to stress. From the point of view of the subject of geography, the most important single fact about the Maoris is the way in which they have become assimilated into the general culture of New Zealand. The head-hunters of New Guinea, if indeed any remain at all, are to be numbered in a few hundred at the most: geographically they have little or no significance in the geography of South East Asia. Similarly, from a geographical point of view, the malaria-carrying mosquito is far more serious a threat than any number of lions, tigers, and other dramatic wild animals.

This division makes the selection of material difficult. The teacher is torn between exciting travellers' tales—seldom typical or indeed accurate—but likely to hold the attention of young children, and the more significant if humdrum facts about other modes of life.

Teachers must accept that television will be followed avidly at home by a very large proportion of young children. Unfortunately it is over the point that is being discussed that television is least helpful. It is quite understandable that a television producer, finding somewhere in France that specialises in rearing edible snails or breeding frogs for their legs, should make a feature about it. It is equally understandable that a teacher should regret that children should come to school after watching the programme with the impression that these commodities are the staples of the French diet and the mainstay of French agriculture.

As with many problems in education there can be but a compromise solution. The teacher can seek for the most striking features that can be regarded as normal. In dealing with fisheries, a teacher can describe life on a trawler in an Arctic gale, since such weather conditions, though by no means normal or usual, are encountered frequently enough to be considered a part of a trawlerman's life. Again, a teacher wishing to bring home to a class ideas about conservation may find it effective to start by talking of whaling and the resulting virtual extinction of the blue whale: at least this is more arresting than dealing with the less exciting, if more serious, threat to wild life posed by an over-use of D.D.T.

The selection of material suitable for the age and ability of children raises other problems. One of these can be illustrated by taking an aspect of environmental study. It is undeniably sound, following modern educational thought, if long term aims involve the children gaining a knowledge and an insight into the geography of the immediate local area. Equally unexceptional is the argument that this should include some knowledge of the work that is undertaken locally. However a hidden difficulty is revealed when it comes to planning individual lessons. There are many schools set near factories, but it often occurs that these factories are not devoted to the simple tasks of baking and candle-stick making, but are places where synthetic resins, industrial belting, electronic testing components, and similar products are produced—none of which can be comprehended by younger children. In such cases an important element in immediate lesson planning is the modification of idealised educational theory to the realities of the classroom.

In addition to selection, planning also involves the rearrangement of material in a way that is suited to the capabilities of a class. The question of rearrangement is important. Taking an example, the savanna grasslands of Africa can support large grass-eating animals in sufficient numbers for large predators to have evolved. The most successful of these is the lion. This is the species best adapted to the environment in strength, hunting ability and camouflage colour. This statement is given in a logical order: an order in which the colour of lions is shown as merely one result of the environment. This is the order in which the information would probably be presented to adults. However with young children, say children of seven years of age, it is often more effective to reverse the order. A large picture of a lion is likely to awaken interest in the minds of the majority of children of this age. A teacher can use such a picture and lead discussion from the colour of the animal to the idea of a countryside that, for much of the year, is tawny-brown and dusty.

A similar argument can be advanced where products are to be studied. A teacher might well decide that a class of eight-year olds should set out to find some information about the bread that they eat. A logical starting point might well be the growing of wheat in the Prairie Provinces of Canada. However many teachers would regard it as preferable, having regard to the age of the children, to start the work by considering the local shop, then asking where the shop keeper obtained his supplies, thus tracing the product back stage by stage from the end product to the raw material: from the shop that the children know back to the source in the wheat belt of Canada. The normal logical working order from start to finish is here reversed in obedience to the old dictum that it is frequently effective to proceed from the known to the unknown.

Just as the order of material must be changed on occasions, so it is often necessary to change units in order to make material suitable for younger children. This is often the case with matters of size and distance simply because many of the measurements dealt with in geography are too large for children to understand. How important this is can be brought out by a simple experiment. Most people know where the Red Sea lies and are sufficiently familiar with the map of the world to place it easily, even though they have done little academic study of geography. It is interesting to ask a group of such people to jot down a figure representing what they believe is the total length of the Red Sea. In the majority of cases, judging from experiments carried out with student teachers, it will be found that they have seriously under-estimated the distance, often giving a figure that is well under a half of the true distance (a little over 1300 miles). The reasons for errors of this kind are not difficult to seek and help our understanding of children's difficulties. First, for most people, distances of this magnitude are somewhat unreal. Such figures are easy enough to handle arithmetically: clearly 1300 miles is more than 1000 miles and less than 2000 miles—but all such distances are lumped together mentally as 'a long way'. Then again most people, asked to estimate the length of the Red Sea, conjure up a mental image of an atlas map of Africa. On this the Red Sea is a tiny strip of blue in the upper right hand corner—and despite all that may be known of scales there is a tendency to underestimate such an area. Possibly too the story of Moses and the Exodus militates against people forming an accurate mental picture of the size of the Red Sea.

Given these difficulties, the problem faced in lesson planning is to decide how such distances may be presented to young children. In the case of the Red Sea a more effective result is obtained by talking in terms of time. An ocean-going passenger vessel is likely to average 400 miles per day. This can be used to present the length of the Red Sea much more strikingly in terms of three days voyage. This can be made even more forceful if the meaning is stressed by the teacher. It means, for instance—a teacher might tell eight-year olds—that a traveller from Aden to Suez will have three breakfasts, three dinners and three teas on board: that if today is Wednesday and we were just leaving the harbour it would be Saturday before the voyage was over.

This teaching technique can be further illustrated by taking an example involving different units. A teacher might well consider it desirable to give a class of ten year olds some idea of the size of London. Now to tell such children that Greater London contains some 10 000 000 people is virtually meaningless. One way out of this difficulty is to work in different units. Assume, a teacher might say, that every person in Greater London wanted just one extra 2 oz. bar of chocolate on a particular day. If this happened the manufacturers would have to send in extra supplies. Working out how much would have to be sent is striking.

$$10\ 000\ 000 \text{ bars would entail } \frac{10\ 000\ 000}{8} = 1\ 250\ 000 \text{ lbs.}$$

Assume (allowing for packing materials and for easy arithmetic) that there are 2000 lbs of chocolate bars in 1 ton of crates to be moved. This gives $\dfrac{1\ 250\ 000}{2000} = 625$ tons.

A delivery lorry can carry ten tons. Thus a convoy of some 63 lorries, enough to jam up the traffic in the road outside the school very effectively, would be needed just to give everyone in Greater London a single bar of chocolate.

So far the problem of planning a lesson has been considered very much from the teacher's view point: from a consideration of what material is suitable, how this material can be arranged and how difficult points can be anticipated and explained. This is, of course, only a part of what planning entails. Equally important is the question as to what the children are to do during the lesson. Indeed a neglect of this section of planning would result in lessons that were over-directed by the teacher.

The decision as to what the children are to do is one that demands careful thought on the part of the teacher. There is certainly no easy solution. If one visits a large number of schools for younger children it is difficult to remain unimpressed by the wide variety of techniques that experienced teachers have devised. To many a teacher in training the variety seems endless and the situation highly confusing.

It is possible, however, to reduce this confusion by codifying the majority of activities into four groups. Figure 1 represents an attempt to produce a model for activities where geography is being taught to younger children.

The first group of methods includes all the forms of teaching that entail telling or showing children something of the subject of the lesson. The children can listen to accounts or stories related by the teacher, or by some outside person through the medium of radio. They can look at pictures, charts, television or film: they can examine objects brought in by the teacher or listen to tape recordings. On the model all these forms of teaching are labelled 'passive'. Since 'passive' is a word with emotional over-tones in education, it must be stressed that excellent results are obtained by these methods. Film, for example, is one of the most powerful of teaching aids. All that is implied by the use of the word 'passive' is that children will spend a considerable proportion of the time watching or listening rather than taking an active part. It is thus desirable, in the light of what is known of the ways

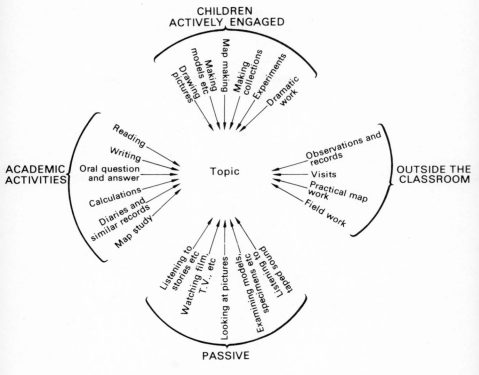

Figure 1   A pattern of possible activities centred on a geographical topic

in which children learn, to balance such work with other activities.

The second group of activities are those in which children are personally engaged in the work. Such activities range widely and include the drawing of pictures, the making of models, and the work of dramatising scenes connected with the theme of the lesson.

A third group of techniques are those involving work that is undertaken outside the classroom: visits to museums, exhibitions, farms and factories. Simple field work is an important element here.

Finally there are those activities that are labelled 'academic' on the model. These are the activities more traditionally associated with schools and scholars. They include encouraging children to read about the subject of the lesson and guiding them to the use of reference books to find additional information. It is in methods belonging to this group that children get practical experience of using the school or the class library. Also included here are all forms of work involving writing or calculating.

The selection of an activity is subject to a number of considerations. Some of these are strictly mundane. Obviously not all activities can be applied to any one given theme. Then again, in a series of lessons on 'things that we drink', there may be excellent film available for coffee but not for tea. It may also happen that there is ample reference material in the school library for work on cocoa but not for coffee. The teacher may have some excellent visual material on tea but not on other beverages. Such utilitarian considerations are inevitable.

Within the limits thus set by circumstances, it is a matter for the teacher to judge what is most suitable, particularly having regard to what the children have been doing in other fields of study.

Commonly, in modern primary school practice, a variety of activities will be selected, thus making it possible for the teacher to prescribe according to the needs of individuals or of groups. This is particularly the case where a considerable period of time, spread over several days, is involved, as will be the case when a teacher decides to expand a theme until it becomes more of the nature of a 'project'.

But whether one or several activities are selected, and whatever the reasons for the selection, the criterion that can be applied to judge the success of a period is easily stated. It is simply a question of the degree to which the initial objective set by the teacher was in fact achieved.

Part 2

Elements of geographical teaching

4

Introducing the tools of geography

'There are some people who do not care for maps: this I find hard to believe.' The quotation is from Robert Louis Stevenson, author of *Treasure Island*, the classic example of a story built up round a map. The comment reveals something of Stevenson's instinctive understanding of children, for the majority of children find a fascination in maps. Evidence of this fascination can be seen both in the care that children lavish on the maps that they prepare themselves, and in the intense interest shown by even very young children if they are given the opportunity of examining a really large and colourful atlas.

As in many matters concerning young children our knowledge of why children are interested in maps is largely empirical: the fact can be observed to be so even if we cannot explain it fully. In part it seems to spring from the fact that children soon link maps with adventure and travel in the adult world. In part, where maps of the child's own local area are involved, there is the fascination of seeing one's own world in miniature. Where children are left free to design their own maps there is the fascination of creating a world to one's own design. Perhaps rather more mundane is the fact that in drawing a map a child finds a satisfaction that comes from achieving exactly what is intended. There is an important step in a child's development that can be overlooked: the stage at which a child becomes aware of his own limitations. Thus if a very young child is asked to draw a cow he does this cheerfully. A little later the same child realises that the 'sausage on sticks' shape is not enough, and also realises that he does not know how to improve it. This is the position that many adults share. With the comfortingly simple lines of many maps problems of this kind do not crop up: it is possible to approach perfection much more easily.

The fact that maps interest children is of fundamental importance in assessing the role of geography in their education since maps are an essential and integral part of geography. Indeed, certainly with children in the middle years of primary education, a geography lesson demands a map (unless the lesson is based directly on the reality outside the classroom). In deference to the age of the children it is pointed out that the word map may here be interpreted very widely to include sand-tray and other models and also those pictorial maps which lie on the border between true maps and pictures.

Despite the interest that children show in maps, care and thought are required in introducing maps to young children. In part this springs from the wide variety of maps in common use, ranging from large scale street plans to small scale maps of whole countries, from simple sketch plans to highly sophisticated cartograms such as those displayed at many bus and railway stations. Although maps are complex the fact that young children can carry out such work is established. Indeed the Schools Council Environmental Studies Project book *Starting from Maps* (Melville Harris, published by Rupert Hart-Davis, 1972) makes the claim that 'most of the basic concepts of maps can, and should, be developed at primary school level'.

As a result of the difficulties that maps impose, a strong argument can be advanced for a graded scheme of map work to be used within schools for young children rather as carefully devised patterns are advocated for the learning of reading. This is not to suggest that all children should move at the same speed in their map work any more than they would be expected to progress at the same speed in learning to read. *New Thinking in School Geography* (D.E.S. pamphlet no. 59) emphasises that children do not conform to a common standard. 'While some can refer to an atlas and use a scale others are still unaware of the names of the major land and sea masses represented on the globe.' It can be argued that it is educationally sound to arrange the work so that children encounter maps of increasing complexity as they pass through the early years of their education. This is really to restate the idea of the so-called 'spiral curriculum' whereby children meet an idea many times, each time with rather more of the idea made evident. Certainly there seems little to be said for the pattern of learning that involves a sudden introduction to quite advanced maps at the beginning of the secondary stage: an introduction often taking the form of very dull lessons on the symbols used on the Ordnance Survey 1″ maps with the symbols carefully copied from the blackboard by the children and subsequently learned for homework.

Some of the difficulties young children encounter in map work may be considered at this point. A basic difficulty is that a map involves a recognition of distances and lengths, and that younger children's interpretation of these ideas may, and often does, differ from the interpretation of older children and adults. Teachers can look for guidance here to what is sometimes referred to as 'the Geneva school' on the development of concepts relating to length and distance. In 1960 Piaget, Inhelder and Szeminska produced an important book, *The Child's Conception of Geometry* (Routledge and Kegan Paul). This book deals, not with maps as such, but with distance and length; both ideas closely linked to map work.

In their book the writers make a clear distinction between distance and length. Length refers to 'filled in' space: the length of sticks for example and, presumably, the length of streets. Distance refers to the linear separation of objects, of 'empty' space.

One experiment, described in chapter three of *The Child's Conception of Geometry*, is particularly relevant to map work. It studied how children judge distance and come to 'conserve' distance. Two model trees were placed on a table. The child was asked if they were 'near one another' or 'far apart'. Then a cardboard screen was placed between the trees. The child was then asked if the trees were still 'as near' or 'as far apart'.

It was found that up to about seven years of age children tended to regard the distance as changed by the placing of the screen. This is relevant to mapping where two objects might well be separated by a third—two houses by a road, two farms by a stream, etc. The findings suggest, as indeed do other experiments, that with young children maps will be topological (that is, objects will be placed in the correct sequence, rather than at the correct distances). It is interesting to note here that one of the most sophisticated maps in common use, the highly stylised map of the London Underground system, uses this technique quite deliberately. Stations are placed at equal intervals along the lines in the correct order but not at intervals relating to the true distances between them.

Another experiment from the same source concerns length. Two parallel rows of matches were presented to children, the matches being arranged in rows. The matches in one of the rows were rearranged to form a series of zig-zags. The children were asked such questions as to whether an ant, walking along each row, would have travelled the same distance. With very young children the idea of similar length was lost when the row was modified, although this was rectified with rather older children. This is clearly relevant to map work: to distances along a curving road for example. It serves as a warning that children are likely to find difficulty over such seemingly obvious matters.

Over the years a number of techniques for introducing map work to younger children have been devised by teachers. One such technique that has proved to have had a considerable measure of success and which has been sufficiently widely used to be described as the conventional approach, involves beginning by drawing a plan of the classroom. This is extended until a plan of the school is drawn, then a plan of the locality and so on. In each succeeding map the scale becomes smaller and so the area shown is extended. Demonstrably the approach achieves a high degree of success. However there are certain drawbacks. It is by no means easy to draw a sketch plan of a room and to draw in, say, thirty six individual tables or eighteen double desks, without crowding the work—as teachers who have made similar sketch plans for the convenience of identifying members of a new class will testify. This is a difficulty that can be overcome by working to scale, but this presupposes that the matter of working to scale

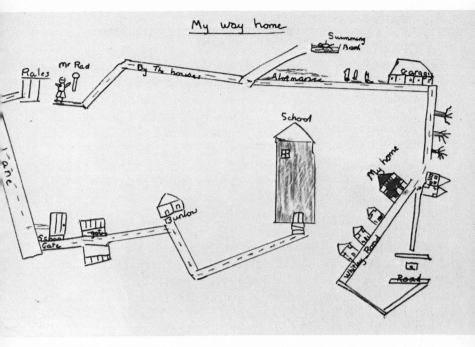

Maps drawn by young children are often partially pictorial. Here the buildings and trees have been shown in profile and such details as the 'lollipop man' at the crossing included. The home, one of a series of identical houses, has been given prominence. In actual fact the home is one of a terrace of 19th century houses, but the child has adopted a typical child's comic form of house. Notice how the scale varies. From the school to the Rales (rails=pedestrian barrier) is only some 100 yards while the total journey is rather over half a mile.

Mr Rad (Read) is the school keeper who does duty as a traffic officer. He lives in the Bunlow (bungalow) within the school grounds.

is fully comprehended by the class. It is demanding much from children to expect them to follow the problems of scale drawing and the concept of a plan simultaneously. Certainly very young children cannot do this. There is a further practical difficulty in that the measurements of a room and its furniture seldom fall in line with the units selected. Thus a scale of 1 cm to 1 metre may be understood, but a table built to the old yard standard does not lend itself to this scale. The arithmetic may well impose such difficulties as to confuse the issue badly.

Mention has already been made of the changes that are taking place in the work presented to younger children at school. One change is that the basic ideas of map work are being introduced to much younger children than was formerly the case. Several infant school teachers claim a considerable measure of success here. Now the maps that such an age group can draw, valuable as they are, inevitably lack the qualities of accuracy that must be present if a plan of a class room is to be recognisable. Such children are experiencing many of the difficulties that Piaget and his colleagues described. The maps of such children are, in fact, a half way stage between true maps and pictures.

Because of the changes that are taking place many schools find it desirable to leave the conventional 'plan of the class room' approach until later; often until the children are nine or ten years of age. At that stage children can handle the mathematics of drawing to scale more readily: the exercise, in fact, becomes a mathematical one but one that also serves as a reinforcement of earlier learning about maps. Other approaches are used with younger children. One approach that has achieved a considerable measure of support is to introduce maps as pictures from above. Following this approach the initial lessons may appear to be little more than a game to the children. A teacher might draw a simple picture on the blackboard: a picture of some common object as it would appear if viewed from directly above. Something of the nature of a tea tray, or a table set for a meal with plates, knives and forks, serves well. The children are invited to halt the teacher as soon as they can guess what is emerging. The game can be played further with, perhaps, the children working in pairs, drawing common objects of all kinds and inviting their partners to guess at the subject of the drawing. Ultimately the teacher can lead the children up to the point where they see a picture of a house or a church as it would appear from above: that is something that is fundamentally a simple map.

An alternative approach that has often proved effective with very young children is to work by way of a model. A typical pattern of work with seven year olds might well be for the children to make a model village. It is emphasised that nothing very elaborate is envisaged here. Buildings can be improvised from boxes and similar scrap materials. In this work an initial step is to establish by class discussion that the village will need houses, shops, a church, etc. These individual buildings can be made by the children, and ultimately arranged on a cardboard base on to which roads have been painted. When the model is complete, and has been admired, the teacher can point out regretfully that it must be packed away for safety. How can it be arranged in the same way tomorrow? How shall we know exactly where to put each building?

With careful questioning along these lines a class can be led to the point where it is suggested that it is easy to draw round the base of each building and label the position of each building.

Of course when this has been done the result is a form of map. This can be 'discovered' under guidance. The teacher may well introduce the idea of the round followed by the local postman, and the children will realise that the round can be followed on the card base without actually taking the trouble of putting the houses back into place. Indeed the base can be pinned up and used as a simple map in a position where it can be seen more conveniently than when it is flat on a table.

It will have been remarked that neither of the approaches described makes mention of scales. The 'pictures from above' game involves nothing more than free-hand drawing. The model is a very simple one without scale calculations. From the purist point of view, the idea of a map without a scale is an anathema, but the omission can be forgiven at this stage. Because a map lacks a written conventional scale or because no scale is

Figure 2 Children's maps often reveal difficulties of perspective, as seen in this section of a seven-year-old's map

expressed when a model is made, does not mean that the idea of proportion is neglected. A skilled teacher will introduce such ideas as the work goes on. 'Here is your house, are you going to add a garden shed?' 'Will it be as big as the house or not?'

Indeed children have some awareness of the ideas of scale from a very early age, as can be noted from their attitude towards toys. Most toy shops stock toy soldiers made to two different scales: 1/72 and 1/32. Children play readily with either, but they seldom mix them in their play. If children are asked about this they will, of course, not answer in technical terms that the items are out of scale: the probable form of words is more likely to be 'those are too big'. However the situation represents an early recognition of the idea of scale. It is interesting to notice that manufacturers have noted this. Where large items are designed to go with figures (tanks for toy soldiers, trees for farm layouts, etc.) a real difficulty of size would occur if these larger items were made to the same true scale as the figures. Instead a proportional scale is used so that the objects still 'look right' in the eyes of a child.

Much more important than the introduction of formal work on scales at this stage is that a young child, once introduced to the basic idea of the nature of a map, should have sufficient practice to clarify these ideas and make them completely familiar. It is to the advantage of a child to be given a variety of work involving maps. This could include such work as the drawing of a simple

With younger children the differences between maps and diagrams such as cross-sections are often blurred. The child who drew this spoke of her 'map'. Notice that the furniture in the right hand bedroom is shown in plan view while other furniture is shown in elevation. Colours were originally used to differentiate the bathroom and toilet—a technique that is really much more sophisticated than that used for the other rooms. The size of the tree compared to the size of the table reveals the problem of scale.

sketch plan of his garden, or it could involve more imaginative work whereby a child could make up maps of imaginary islands.

During such practice map work, young children often show, by the nature of the mistakes that they make, where difficulties lie. A very common error is for children to show such features as roads correctly, but to show houses in profile rather than in plan. An example of this is given in figure 2. Such errors serve as a reminder that comprehension of the nature of a map must involve the ability to visualise land from an unusual standpoint: from immediately above, looking downwards.

Piaget and Inhelder have reported experiments that involved problems similar in nature. Thus in one test children were shown a group of three model mountains. Each was easily identifiable since one had a cross on top, the second a model house, while the third had snow painted on it. Then a doll was added to the group and the children had to select drawings depicting what the doll would see, since, of course, the doll would be viewing the group from a different angle from the child. The experiment revealed that very young children found this to be beyond them. They tended to select the picture that showed the view that they themselves saw. This difficulty with perspective is very similar to the difficulty that occurs in mapping, where a child has to look at a house from ground level and try to visualise its form when seen from above.

It is interesting to note, incidentally, that when a child draws a house in profile rather than in plan view on a map, the child is, unknowingly, following a convention of mapping that persisted in adult maps up into the eighteenth century. Villages, towns, and even hills were often shown in profile in early maps. Even the modern 1″ Ordnance Survey maps, in the choice of symbols used for windmills, windpumps and wireless or television masts, follows the same tradition. The symbols used are basically little drawings of the objects as seen from the ground.

Having established the fundamental idea of a map, a teacher

A section from an Ordnance Survey sheet (scale 50 inches to 1 mile). Here a whole school is included on one sheet: buildings and playing fields can be easily identified.

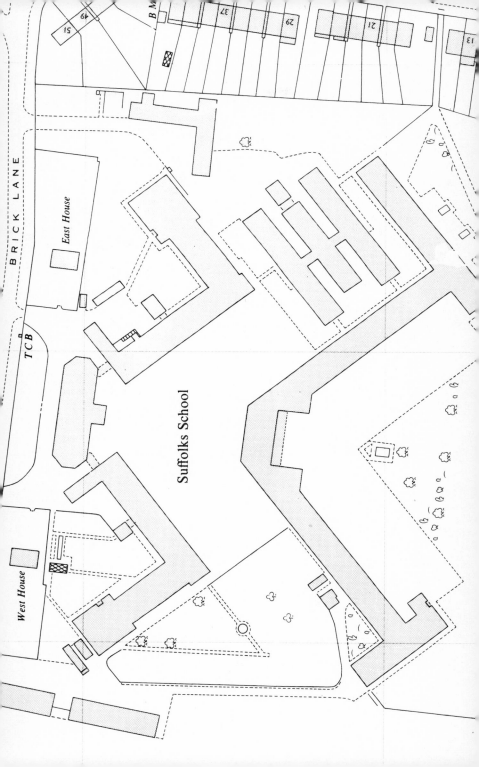

will wish to progress from this point. Two progressions can be noted here. The first maps that a child will handle will include a large proportion of maps of the immediate local area. At first these will be very simple maps indeed. A teacher will wish to increase the amount of detail, not only to increase the child's appreciation of mapping, but also so that maps of the locality can be used to record information about the local environment. In this context the recently introduced Ordnance Survey sheets (for urban areas only) at a scale of 50 inches to the mile are invaluable since at this exceptionally large scale a wealth of detail is possible. As published the maps are printed in black and white, but greater clarity can be given by colouring them.

The second type of progression is also of importance. Initially a child will be handling a large scale map of the local area. Here the map, something new and unfamiliar, represents an area that is very well known indeed. In fact, during the early stages, the child is not so much reading the map as using his knowledge of the area to decipher the map. With increasing familiarity with maps the process can be reversed, and the situation created whereby a London child can examine a large scale map of somewhere that is quite unfamiliar, such as a Welsh mining village, and appreciate a great deal of what the unfamiliar place is like.

It will be noticed that so far nothing has been said of the matter of orienting the map or of using a north pointer. Initially these are probably unnecessary complications. With very large scale sketch plans involving only a few familiar streets at the most, a north pointer is not required. Ideas of this kind come later and are discussed later in this book. A beginning can be made by a teacher talking of a main road that is familiar to the class, and drawing a simple map of this road on paper pinned to the floor. The map can be really simple: little more than a pair of parallel lines, roughly oriented, is required. The teaching can then take the form of questioning. 'If we were to travel along this road, where would we come to?' 'Where would we reach after that?' Thus when children have begun to grasp the idea of direction to the next district, the direction of other districts can be established. At this early stage of map work this is frequently sufficient.

5
Extending the use of the tools

The problems that maps present to younger children are exceedingly complex, and the introduction of maps calls for considerable skill on the part of the teacher.

The previous chapter gave some indication of the problems of introducing maps. However within the primary stage teachers will wish to advance the children's skills beyond the initial standards already discussed. The argument that this should be done by a scheme of map work that ensures that children encounter maps in a carefully graded order of difficulty is here further advanced.

A possible scheme for map work within the primary stage is indicated by the flow-diagram in figure 3. The left hand side of the figure summarises the earlier contention: that maps should be introduced in the form of large scale maps of the familiar home locality. Such large scale maps, increasing in detail as children become more familiar with the conventions of mapping, are of value throughout the primary stage. Indeed the utility of such maps in education extends well beyond this stage, for such maps have their value in secondary and even higher education. That this is so is indicated by the arrow in the diagram.

A particular use of such maps is as base maps on which information and records collected by the children themselves can be marked. A second progression, one that has already been discussed, is from large scale maps of the home area to large scale maps of areas that are not known to the children.

Useful though large scale maps are in the geographical education of young children, the time comes when maps showing larger areas are needed. Schools are fortunate in this country in

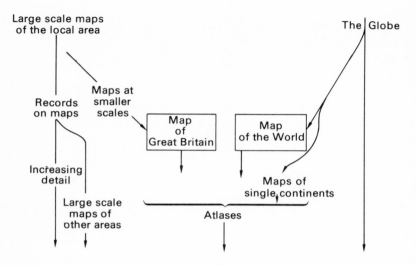

Figure 3 A possible scheme for mapwork within the primary stage

that a complete series of maps with decreasing scales is available
from the Ordnance Survey. The largest of all scales, the 50 inches
to 1 mile plans, have already been mentioned. Next in the series
is the 25 inches to 1 mile, a series that is admirable when, for
example, a plan of the local main shopping centre is required.
The 6 inches to 1 mile series follows, giving, at this reduced scale,
a much wider coverage. Where schools are fortunate enough to
find that the school buildings fall towards the centre of such
sheets, it will be found that in most areas the whole school
catchment area is contained within a single sheet. Following the
maps available down the scales, the next scale is 1:25 000 (about
$2\frac{1}{2}$ inches to 1 mile). At this scale a single sheet will show the
whole of a moderately large town, together with the roads
leading to it and the surrounding suburbs and villages. The
familiar 1 inch to 1 mile map is next, followed by the $\frac{1}{4}$ inch to
1 mile—a scale at which a single sheet will show the whole of
South Wales or all of the area of London and the south-east
coast of England. The series published by the Ordnance Survey
culminates in the 1:625,000 series (about 1 inch to 10 miles) in
which the whole of Great Britain is covered in two sheets.

This is a very important series indeed at any stage of education: a really full range of maps showing many facets of Britain. For junior school pupils the general topographic map is the most suitable, offering what is probably the finest (as well as the cheapest large wall map of Great Britain available anywhere.

This particular series has great merit in the degree of detail that is shown. It is puzzling and indeed frustrating for a child to spend a summer holiday at, say, a huge holiday camp such as Butlin's at Bognor, and then, on returning to the classroom, to find that Bognor is not marked, presumably because the map maker considered it too small for inclusion. To the child Bognor is not a small place however: to find that it is not marked is disturbing.

A further advantage of the 1:625 000 series is that the Ordnance Survey, by very shrewd use of printing techniques, have produced a map which gives detail without appearing to be cluttered. From across a classroom the map appears bold and clear. If examined at normal reading distance however, the detail can be followed without difficulty and even small villages identified clearly. Admittedly the print size made necessary for minor details by the scale of the map is smaller than one would advise for younger children, but the majority seem to be able to handle this difficulty, particularly when they are looking for the position of a name with which they are already familiar.

Once the map of Great Britain is introduced, it becomes a key teaching aid in many fields of work, hence the prominence given to it in the diagram. If it is placed so that it is readily accessible, a teacher can indicate any place mentioned in any lesson. It is stressed that a brief indication is enough: no one would suggest that every lesson should be turned into a geography lesson. Nevertheless, if the Battle of Hastings is mentioned, it is helpful if the teacher points to the position of Hastings, rather as many teachers will also write the word on the blackboard to indicate the spelling. This use of maps in passing, as it were, has its own intrinsic value in that it has the effect of making children aware that maps can be used as general reference aids, rather as dictionaries are used.

So far this chapter has dealt with the possible progressions that can be followed from large scale maps of the familiar local area, but map work can be approached from a second direction. The two approaches are not offered as alternatives, rather is it suggested that the two complement each other.

This second approach, indicated on the right hand side of the diagram, is by way of the globe.

Here, let it be admitted immediately, is a more controversial matter. There are many educationists who will argue that the presentation of the earth as a ball is too difficult a concept for young children. This is a view that can be argued convincingly, but which still does not appear to be fully justified in practice. Certainly children cannot grasp all the implications of this idea. However there are two factors that must be taken into consideration. It is unwise to underestimate the effect of science fiction as it is presented in children's comics and on television. It must also be remembered that the present generation of children represent the first group to have seen, by way of the cameras carried on the Apollo missions, the majesty of the entire earth rising above the lunar horizon.

Following this up a globe then becomes a vital and important piece of equipment; something that can be used very frequently to indicate where distant places lie, rather as the map of Great Britain can be used for places within this country. Again the degree of comprehension on the part of the children may be queried, but at least it can be argued that familiarity with the globe will lead ultimately to a familiarity with the basic distribution of land and sea: that the pattern will become familiar.

In the classroom a globe with a prepared blackboard surface is probably the most effective, since features marked on it with coloured chalk stand out sharply, the contrasting colours emphasising the matters that are being considered. Such a globe does not give detail, but any detail that is required can be looked for on maps. Some teachers find it effective to keep a small globe (often one of the inexpensive pressed-tin variety) with the class library so that children may refer to it in very much the same way that they refer to reference books.

The essential familiarity with the pattern of the globe that is the aim of this teaching can best be achieved if the teacher devises activities that are linked to it. Such material is often most convenient if it is in the form of puzzles or problems, set out on cards. One of these can be chosen by any child who happens to have finished a piece of work and who is, for a few minutes, without an occupation. Such prepared cards might bear the outline of a single continent or, rather more difficult and therefore something of a progression, a single country. The child's task is to find on the globe the piece of land corresponding to the shape on the card, to identify it, and to hand in the name written on a slip of paper. Subsequently the idea of relative size can be introduced with the cards bearing two outlines, drawn to different scales. Here the child is required to find the two areas and say which is truly the larger. Distances may be considered, using flexible rulers made by the children themselves. These rulers need be no more elaborate than strips of tough card. The children can graduate their own rulers by holding them against a master copy prepared by the teacher. Generally distances of 500 and 1000 km. are the most convenient.

Even a simple piece of string can become a valuable teaching aid when applied to a globe. Stretched tightly across the globe's surface, a string will indicate a 'great circle' route: that is the shortest distance between any two points on the surface. The children's puzzle cards can here include questions about the shortest routes between places, the names of the countries and seas that are crossed, and indeed questions such as finding the shortest route from Australia to Britain—does this lie by way of Panama or by way of Cape Town?

Unfortunately a globe is cumbersome, and children can appreciate that if a globe is 'skinned' and the skin laid out flat— that is if a map of the world is used instead—the result is far more convenient.

Here a difficulty arises. It is mathematically impossible to show the entire surface of a sphere on a flat surface without distortion of some kind. Indeed a whole branch of geography—the science of map projections—has grown up to provide compromise solutions

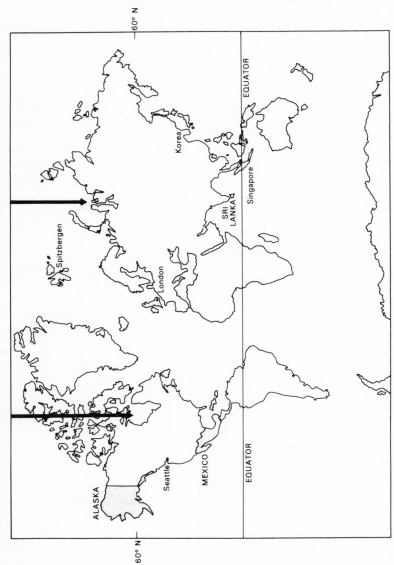

Figure 4 A world map drawn to Mercator's projection

to this fundamental difficulty. It cannot be stressed sufficiently that some map projections are totally unsuited to the needs of young children. In this group are many of the cylindrical projections, including Mercator's.

It is perhaps justifiable to examine the Mercator projection here in some detail, to see why it is so unsuitable for young children. This is necessary since, to many adults whose studies have been in fields other than geography, this projection gives the conventional and customary world map: the map that they see if they close their eyes and try to conjure up an image of a world map.

The world, on Mercator's projection, is shown in figure 4. The mathematics behind this map may be outlined briefly. Since the map is rectangular all the meridians are shown as being the same length: this is, of course, correct. However all the parallels of latitude are also shown as being the same length, which is false. The length of the parallels decreases north and south of the equator. Thus the length of the equator can be calculated as $2\pi R$. (R = radius of the earth.) Parallel 60°N or S will be $2\pi R \cos 60°$. Since the cosine of 60° $= \frac{1}{2}$, then the length of parallel 60° will be πR: that is only half the length of the equator.

However it is shown on the map as being the same length as the equator. This means that the scale of the map has been increased two-fold as compared with the equatorial scale. By itself this would result in a map that appeared to be 'pulled out sideways', so, to avoid this, the scale at 60°N or S is also doubled in a north to south direction. Thus correct shape is preserved at the expense of scale.

This alteration of scale presents two major problems to anyone using a Mercator world map. It is, for example, very difficult indeed to measure the distance between two places, unless they both happen to lie at exactly the same latitude. On the map reproduced here Mexico and Alaska are both shaded. There is little doubt what a child would give as an answer if asked which of these two countries is the nearer to London. In actual fact Alaska is markedly nearer to London than Mexico. The second problem presented to anyone using such a world map is that the doubling of scale in both directions by latitude 60°N or S results in a situation where one square centimetre of paper at the equator represents exactly the same area of land as four square centimetres at 60°, and that this exaggeration becomes even more marked further towards the poles. Any land areas near the equator are shown as absurdly small compared with those near the poles. On the map illustrated here Spitzbergen and Sri Lanka are both marked. Both these are virtually identical in area, but this is certainly not the impression given by the map.

The Mercator projection was originally devised because it has certain real advantages when used for navigation (a point that does not concern the education of young children). The standard world Mercator, as illustrated here, had the advantage that shipping routes could be shown clearly since most such routes run in an east-west direction. However the coming of aviation and satellites has changed this pattern, and many flight paths cross the polar regions. The impossibility of showing the shortest route between the U.S.S.R. and Canada is indicated on the map.

The importance of presenting children with a pattern of land and sea that is free from the fallacies inherent in such projections as Mercator's must be stressed. Inevitably places spring to importance as a result of events: places often not mentioned during a school career because they were not then important. How many of the soldiers who fought at El Alamein had heard of this place while at school? How many Americans who served at Da Nang had had it mentioned to them when they were young? This is not to condemn schools and school teaching, but merely to point out an inevitable process. However it is to be hoped that the geography taught in schools will help the pupils, when they grow up, to appreciate the geographical importance of places as they spring into prominence as a result of world events. That this has not always been so was demonstrated by the difficulty many people had in comprehending a statement that was made about the Korean War. It was pointed out that Korea is on a direct route between the two bases of Singapore and Seattle, and roughly half way between them. People brought up on Mercator's world map found this virtually incomprehensible. The places are marked on the map reproduced here. Readers are invited to compare what is shown

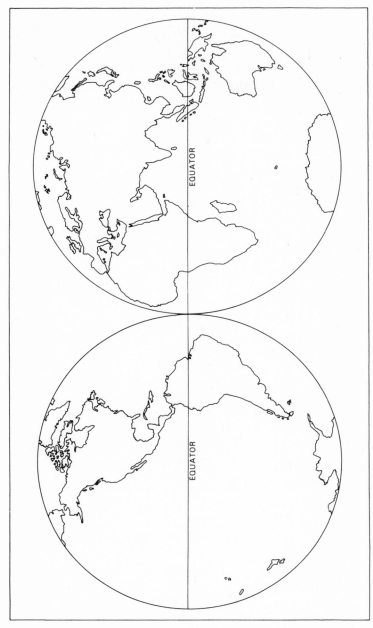

Figure 5   The world divided into two conventional hemispheres

there with what is revealed by the realities of a globe.

The strategic position of Korea seems a very far cry from the geography that is presented to young children. No one suggests that such a point should be made to such an audience. However in helping children to form an image of the world it is important not to confuse future issues by allowing their ideas to form round a model that is likely to mislead.

What then can be offered? Probably the least misleading map is one based on two hemispheres. When only a very small part of the world's surface is represented on a map, the distortion is negligible. The larger the area represented, the greater the inaccuracy until, with a complete world map, distortion becomes

Figure 6   The earth 'tilted' to show Britain in a central position

serious. By using hemispheres the problem becomes less acute, since each half of the map represents only half the earth surface. Further it is possible to alert children to some degree to expect distortion. If a world map, made up of two hemispheres, is presented to young children in terms of the earth 'squashed flat' there is a degree of expectation that the shape will have altered.

The conventional hemispheres involved a division of the earth from pole to pole, as shown in figure 5. This is helpful as a map. However a hemisphere in which the earth is 'tilted', showing Britain in a central position, has many advantages, particularly in the way in which it shows the relationships between North America and Europe. This is shown in figure 6.

Where a single sheet world map is needed, probably Mollweide's projection is the best general map for younger children. This projection achieves a reasonable measure of compromise between distortion of shape, size and scale, and is fairly easily comprehensible (see figure 7).

Given that children have had a careful introduction to map work and that they have engaged in sufficient activities to be at ease with maps, atlases pose few problems. They are, after all, no more than collections of maps bound together for convenience. They are reference books as dictionaries or encyclopedias are reference books and can be used as such. Indeed wise teachers encourage the use of atlases just as the use of any reference book is encouraged, making no distinction between atlases and the other books that are available.

It is worth pointing out, however, the advantage of a school library including at least one large atlas. The *Reader's Digest Great World Atlas* is particularly valuable here since the cartographic techniques used result in very colourful and striking maps that hold a fascination for many children. One special strength of this atlas lies in the way in which relief is shown. It is very difficult for children to read three dimensional detail from a two dimensional map. Indeed any attempt to introduce contour lines is probably best left till the secondary stage. Where conventional layer colouring is met in atlases this is probably best treated as a simple symbol —yellow stands for hills, brown for mountains. The *Reader's*

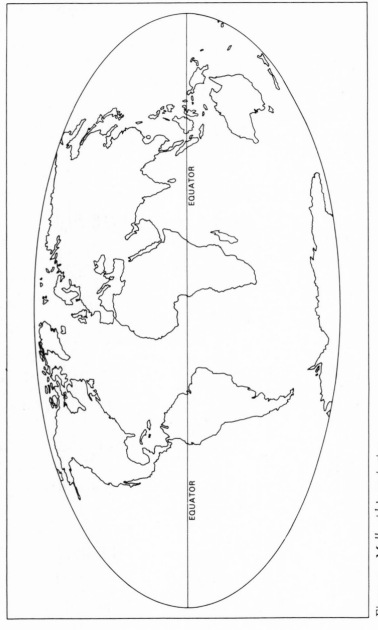

Figure 7 Mollweide's projection

Digest atlas uses a form of representation of relief that gives an immediate visual impression of differing levels. This techinque was developed many years ago by Dr H. Haack whose wall maps are now marketed by Pergamon Press. The general world wall map in this series is especially suited to the needs of upper juniors.

6

Specific skills

Geography, as a study, involves the acquisition of skills. Some of these may be regarded as general skills: skills that may well be increased by the study of geography but which are not confined to it. Thus if younger children are encouraged to write about something geographical that has caught their attention, be it whaling in the Antarctic or the way in which houses are being built on a neighbouring estate, they are likely to acquire additional skill with words. However a skill with words, though obviously essential to geography, is not simply a geographical matter. It is something that is involved in virtually every aspect of the curriculum of a school. On the other hand there are some skills that are so intimately connected with geography that they may be considered specifically linked with the subject. An ability to read a map comes into this category, even though maps may be used in other aspects of the curriculum (in history, perhaps, to show the position of Hastings and the campaigns of William, or in religious education to show the wanderings of the Israelites under Moses).

Maps are sufficiently important to have merited separate treatment, but certain other skills can be discussed here. The group of skills involved in a knowledge of direction may be considered here. Although seemingly a simple idea, the comprehension of the meaning of north, south, east and west is not an easy matter for young children.

An analysis of the problems facing any child attempting to understand the four main direction points reveals some of the complications. First it is not easy for a child to appreciate that north is always the same direction irrespective of where he stands. (Technically this is not true. If a child moves east or west, the direction from the child to the Pole will have changed. This, however, is a much later stage that can be considered with the help of the globe. At all events the difference is hardly measurable for the scale of movement that the child normally undertakes.)

The constancy of a northerly direction differs from the usual experience of young children. Children know, for example, the direction of their school from their home, but they also know that it is possible to walk on past the school, in which case it lies in a different direction. To a young child the understanding of the direction in which the school lies poses few problems, but north is a vaguely comprehended place of Polar Bears with possible Eskimoes and even Father Christmas, while the direction south is equally vague.

A second group of difficulties occur when maps are introduced. It is conventional to draw maps so that north is at the top of the page and there is the natural confusion between 'north' and 'top'. Once established this confusion persists right into adult life. Exactly how complicated this may prove can be gauged when it is recalled that many schools teach upper juniors about Scott of the Antarctic. If a map of Antarctica is used to illustrate the lesson, as is often the case, the children are suddenly faced with a map in which south is in the middle and north is any direction from the centre of the page towards any of the four sides!

Closely linked with this is the problem of associating north on the map with north as it is on the ground. Most adults can close their eyes and conjure up a mental image of the map of Great Britain. For most people this image is based on a school-room wall map or an atlas map. The image is not oriented in any way except in the sense that north is at the top.

Even where north and south are established clearly there is still the problem of east and west. Investigation undertaken with adult geography students reveals that there is still a substantial proportion of such people who experience a slight hesitation in differentiating between the two directions: a confusion that has its beginnings in very early geography teaching. The difficulties that children meet can be compared with the problem of learning left from right: a matter that can confuse some children until late in the primary stage if not beyond. The two matters are probably linked because of the convention of putting north at the top. 'Up' and 'down' are learned more quickly than 'left' and 'right'. Similarly north and south are learned more easily than east and west.

There is, unfortunately, no one approach to the whole matter of teaching the skills involved in handling matters of direction. This is not a counsel of despair, but rather an intimation that the whole matter is not something that can be dealt with in a single group of lessons and then dismissed as known. Obviously striking and extremely valuable lessons are given on this topic. To give examples, an upright stick will cast a shadow in a north-south line at noon: a line that can be marked permanently and named. The same shadow device at sunset will give an indication of east and west. (Technically there are only two days in the year when this is true: when the sun rises and sets due east and west. However the error involved at other times is too slight to be significant at this stage.) The results obtained by studying shadows can be compared with the behaviour of a compass, and a compass made available on the 'discovery table' in the classroom. The whole of this work can be reinforced by games in the playground, when children 'run north' or 'run east' to commands. A semi-permanent reminder can be marked up in the classroom or on the playground surface.

But even when such work is undertaken the fundamental problems remain and need attention even with older pupils. It is, for example, interesting with older juniors to select one of the four points of the compass and ask them to face in that direction and imagine what they would see if they were able to board a helicopter and fly in a completely straight line. Taking London children for example, and assuming that north is chosen, the helicopter would take off and then fly very much along the line of the valley of the River Lea, with the great reservoirs that supply London lying beneath. It would cross the line of the East Anglian Heights near Bishop's Stortford, and then pass on, with Cambridge a few miles to the right. The flight would just skirt the westermost corner of the Wash, and then cross the Humber estuary very near Grimsby. The last sight of Britain would be the long low coast of Holderness in Yorkshire.

This exercise can be made even more vivid an exercise in using geography imaginatively by extending it to include the world as a whole.

This ability to think in terms of the globe as a whole is a skill that reveals itself in other ways. At a very early age children will accept the idea that the earth is a sphere. It has already been argued that comics, accounts of space travel and even the B.B.C. television interval signal have contributed to this. However all these leave the child in the position of an observer in space, stationary as far as the earth is concerned, watching the earth rotate before him. What is far more difficult for a child to visualise is that he is actually standing upon a rotating sphere. This is the problem that occurs when an attempt is made to explain such a phenomenon as day and night. This can be demonstrated in a variety of ways: for example, with a light for the sun and the classroom globe to represent the earth. It can be shown by films or by film loops: all material that is easily available to schools. But even when these aids are used, the children are still in the position of an external observer. They are not really being helped to comprehend the idea of standing on a rotating earth that is turning towards a rising sun. Because of this difficulty it is probably unduly optimistic for a teacher to expect much real comprehension of the reasons behind day and night until at least the upper junior stage, and there is no need to worry unduly if comprehension does not come, even with able children, until well into the secondary stage. This is not to say that the matter should not be mentioned. Indeed children will meet the idea very early, if only from finding that sports fixtures in the United States or Australia are broadcast at what seem very strange times of day indeed as far as they are concerned.

When the difficulties associated with the rotation of the earth are considered, it becomes apparent that the even more complex pattern of the earth's rotation round the sun, with all the phenomena of the seasons, the 'midnight sun', etc., is even less likely to be comprehended by any but the most able children in the upper junior stage. This is not to be interpreted to mean that children gain nothing of this knowledge. Their position is, however, much more that of gathering the data that they will ultimately need for these ideas to be comprehended. Thus a classroom globe is normally manufactured with the axis at an angle. Children do not usually question this, but the fact that they grow accustomed to seeing the globe set at an angle in this fashion ultimately makes it easier for them to comprehend the basic cause of the seasons. (It seems a pity, incidentally, that manufacturers do not include a simple rachet mechanism in school globes so that children do not also become familiar with the right and wrong direction in which the earth rotates.)

If work with young children is thus of the nature of gathering data, it is clearly the responsibility of teachers to ensure that the relevant data is noticed, even though the reasons may not be explained. For example, even with very young children in the infant stage changes in the length of daylight can be noted, with the children encouraged to remember, during the autumn term, which was the first day when it was necessary to put on the lights before afternoon school finished, or, in the spring, when it first became possible to have breakfast without putting on the light. Where children are learning to tell the time, they can practise this new skill with lighting-up times as they are published in the newspapers. All this material has its own intrinsic interest to young children. Its full educational value is shown as the children, with growing knowledge and maturity, develop the special skill of being able to form an accurate mental image of the moving earth.

A completely new set of skills is involved when children are encouraged to begin to think along specifically geographical lines. The Plowden Report suggests that there are three broad stages through which children pass in their geographical education in the primary school. At first, in the infant stage, the children are concerned with indiscriminate examination and observation of objects, events and phenomena. In the second stage, the continued enlargement of vocabulary is accompanied by more discriminating and selective examination, in which single objects or phenomena are isolated and analysed. Finally, in the third stage, the analysis and comparison of phenomena take on precision as mathematical skills, language, and simple argument come to be employed.

To think in terms of these three stages is helpful in considering the problem of how to guide children so that they develop the skill of thinking along geographical channels. The Plowden Report gives as an example some work done by infants, where a walk out of doors was recorded on a large wall frieze in which houses, the church, trees, clouds, a lorry driver and a dog were all prominently depicted. Three-dimensional models were made and some words, phrases and sentences written to accompany the pictorial record. This is typical of the kind of work that children in the first stage undertake. The particular responsibility of the teacher here is to guide children's observation and channel their interest so that their attention is drawn to significant points: to matters that can be explored in more detail later. The lorry driver, mentioned above, is a case in point. Here, in a driver and his lorry, is something so familiar that it can easily be ignored by children. Yet there is educational value here. During the first early stage it may be enough for the children to note where the driver sits, the colour of the lorry, how many wheels it has, and similar points. This will probably be sufficient. Subsequently, in the second stage, lorries might well be a theme studied in much more detail by a group of children. Here the different types of lorries might be noted, the ways in which lorries are specially adapted to carry differing loads, the fact that lorries often show the location of the owners and the type of business involved. In the final stage, in the upper junior school, the same theme can be studied again, this time with much greater precision. A simple road census can be undertaken, with children noting the number and type of vehicles passing a given point in a fixed time and recording the results in a simple block graph. The loads can be noted, and a reason found for the predominance of certain loads. (For example, a familiar sight on many Hertfordshire roads are car transporters taking new vehicles from Luton towards the London docks.)

This three-fold development can be further illustrated in terms of weather study. With very young children (in the first stage of development as suggested by Plowden) weather is linked with many other things. 'We went to Whipsnade and it was hot and we saw lions and had sandwiches for lunch.' Accounts of this kind reflect this haphazard pattern of examination and recording. However weather study is sufficiently important to be singled out for careful study throughout the primary stage.

Figure 8 represents an attempt to construct a model to show how weather skills can be developed throughout the primary stage. The left hand side of this figure suggests the work that can be undertaken from the early years of the infants' stage to the final year of the junior school. Thus, from a starting point of purely indiscriminate observation, children in the infant stage can progress to a very simple record noting the weather at the time of observation. This can be done in the simple form sketch shown at (*a*): no more than a card requiring a word and a picture to be added. Although this is a very simple device, two goals can be achieved here. First, as the work progresses, more precise terms can be introduced, including such ideas as the difference between mist and fog. A wider vocabulary is introduced here to describe temperature. (Very young children tend to over-use the terms 'hot' and 'cold', rather as they over-simplify characters seen on television as 'goodies' and 'badies'. Words such as 'warm', 'chilly', and 'mild' can be introduced at this stage.) The second aim of this particular piece of work is for the children to progress from drawing a little picture illustrative of weather conditions to adding something approaching a symbol (e.g. an umbrella for rain). This is a useful preparation for subsequent work.

As children progress towards the second stage mentioned in the Plowden Report, towards the point where weather is more specifically selected for study, more detailed analysis is needed. Here a chart similar to that shown at (*b*) can be employed. Under these circumstances children spend a few minutes twice a day looking at the weather and putting their observations on record. The importance of this step is that the children can begin to appreciate that weather follows regular sequences. A bright

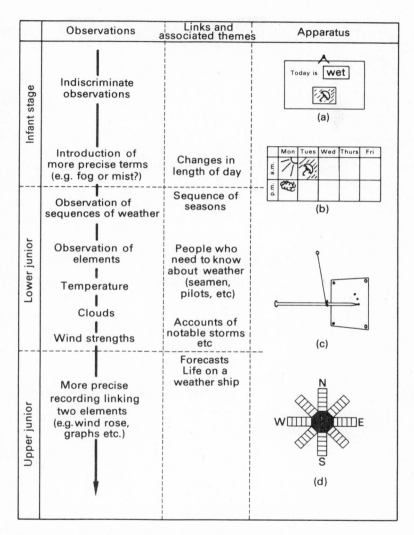

	Observations	Links and associated themes	Apparatus
Infant stage	Indiscriminate observations		Today is wet (a)
	Introduction of more precise terms (e.g. fog or mist?)	Changes in length of day	
Lower junior	Observation of sequences of weather	Sequence of seasons	Mon Tues Wed Thurs Fri a.m. p.m. (b)
	Observation of elements	People who need to know about weather (seamen, pilots, etc)	(c)
	Temperature		
	Clouds		
	Wind strengths	Accounts of notable storms etc	
Upper junior	More precise recording linking two elements (e.g. wind rose, graphs etc.)	Forecasts Life on a weather ship	N W E S (d)

Figure 8   Weather recording in the primary stage

67

morning that becomes more and more humid until, finally, a thunderstorm breaks is a sequence that is familiar enough to adults, but not necessarily familiar to seven-year olds.

This analysis of weather can be taken more deeply by examining the elements that make up weather and observing them in more detail. Temperature may be taken first and records kept. Initially the four words 'hot', 'warm', 'mild' and 'cold' may be sufficient for the children to describe temperatures, but it is not long before a situation is reached where genuine disagreement is found among a group of children as to which word is most suitable for a given observation. At this point a thermometer can be introduced and used. Similarly cloud types can be noted and marked on a chart, together with a word or two recording the weather experienced with each type. Here a simple five-fold classification of clouds is enough: cumulus, cirrus, stratus, nimbus and clear skies. Wind directions can be recorded, using an improvised wind stocking, and also wind strengths, using a simplified version of the official Beaufort scale.

Rainfall can be observed and recorded, although attempts to measure the amount of rainfall in millimetres are seldom very successful at this stage, largely because the actual amounts involved, in all but exceptional circumstances, are too small to be measured except with a properly designed rain gauge. An alternative that has proved effective is to pin a sheet of coloured blotting paper to a board and to hold this out in the rain for five seconds—while a class counts to five slowly. The rain drops mark the blotting paper, leaving a record that can be made permanent by drawing round the drops with a ball-point pen. If this is done on three or four separate occasions the children have an immediate visual impression of the difference between drizzle, light rain, and heavy thundery rain: an impression based both on the size of the raindrops and their frequency.

An omission will be noted in these suggestions for the analysis of weather. At this stage it is probably desirable not to introduce the idea of pressure. Although pressure changes figure largely in official forecasts, pressure is a difficult idea for young children since the changes of pressure involved in weather changes are too slight to be sensed by the human body. All the other elements mentioned can be sensed: pressure cannot.

As children develop towards the third stage mentioned by the Plowden Report other skills can be brought into play. For instance children can carry out simple experiments. The apparatus necessary for one such experiment is indicated at (c). A lightweight knitting needle is held against a wall by resting one end of it on a pin. The needle is supported in a position roughly parallel to the floor by a single long human hair. Since human hair expands and contracts according to the humidity of the atmosphere, the point of the needle will indicate these changes. A record of previous positions can be marked on a sheet of paper pinned to the wall behind the needle.

A second experiment might demonstrate the condensation of atmospheric water vapour on the sides of a jar that is cooled by placing some cold water and a few ice cubes inside. The presence of water droplets on the side of the jar can be shown by wiping the sides of the jar with coloured blotting paper which changes colour when wet.

By this stage of their work, primary children are capable of following the scientific reasoning behind these experiments.

At this stage children can also use simple mathematical techniques. Graphs of many kinds can be drawn. The children can also use the 'wind rose' type of weather chart, shown at (d). This has the advantage that two elements in weather can be recorded together (e.g. wind direction and temperature). If such a chart is maintained until quite a number of observations have become available, children can use their mathematics to express such ideas as the proportion of days with an east wind that are also cold.

A totally different set of skills come into play when pictures are considered. Although pictures are used as teaching material in a very wide range of school activities indeed, there are specific skills in the interpretation of pictures to deduce geographical points.

These skills are more than sheer accuracy of observation, important though this is. It is a matter of learning how to look for significant causal relationships. A young child, shown a picture of a crowded city street, can be encouraged to make observations. These, with the majority of young children, will be unrelated to each other. 'That man has an umbrella.' 'That woman has a brown overcoat.' 'The little boy has a scarf.' An older child who has developed skills in deductive observation along geographical lines will say: 'It is winter because the people have coats, scarves and umbrellas.'

Picking out what is significant in a picture and using the facts gained to draw conclusions is a skill that children can develop to a surprisingly high degree given both guidance and patience. This skill results when pictures are used as specific teaching aids rather than as mere illustrations. Thus a picture of, say, a village in south Germany can be glanced at with very much the same superficial attention that children give to many television programmes in the home. Alternatively the same picture can become the centre of specific teaching. This might involve drawing the attention of the children to the traditional type of roof found in southern Germany, and helping them to see a link between the heavy roofs with the characteristic overhanging eaves and the heavy snowfall of the area. It is this need for the detailed study of pictures that robs some lessons based on filmstrips of their value. It is commercially impracticable to manufacture a filmstrip with fewer than some thirty frames, but this does not mean that the whole strip has to be flashed across a screen in a single lesson. At this speed it is difficult indeed for children to develop skills in interpreting pictures.

There is also the skill with pictures that involves using a number of pictures to build up a synoptic view. Thus a teacher dealing with the Canadian northlands will wish to show the class pictures illustrating the bitter winters of these areas. Yet this is not enough. Children also need to see pictures showing these lands during the brief but surprisingly hot summers, when flowers bloom in the tundra, and when insects thrive to such an extent that they prove a real nuisance to both man and beast. The children need to see pictures of both, and to have the main points brought out, if they are to gain practice of using the pictures to build up a balanced image of the whole pattern.

The school shown in this aerial photograph is the same as that on the large scale (50 inches to 1 mile) Ordnance Survey map reproduced on page 45.

The fact that this is not as easy as it sounds is reflected in the way in which some children, having had the idea that the tundra is very cold impressed on their minds very thoroughly, will reject a picture of the tundra's summer flowers as false. They cannot accommodate the new idea (using the word here as Piaget does to indicate a modification of existing beliefs to accommodate new material) since they have not been encouraged to use pictures to make comparisons.

Closely linked with the interpretation of pictures generally is the skill involved in the interpretation of aerial photographs. Here tremendous changes have taken place. Aerial photographs were, at one time, considered very difficult for young children to comprehend. Now they are widely used in many books and there is little evidence to suggest that children find them difficult. A distinction must be made here between high level photographs taken vertically (the type of photograph used in making surveys) and low level photographs taken at an oblique angle. The first type does present difficulty, even to adults, while the second does not. Particularly when used in conjunction with maps, low-level oblique photographs have a real value in teaching.

7
General skills

Despite all that has been said and written about changes in the primary school curriculum and about near revolutionary changes in our approaches to the problem of educating young children, few teachers would dissent from the statement that the primary stage is intimately concerned with primary skills. An earlier generation of teachers spoke of the 'three R's'—reading, 'riting, and 'rithmetic—and gave these studies pride of place in school timetables. Our interpretation of the three R's is much wider; our attitude to children's development has altered; our ideas of the purpose of schools have changed. Yet it is still true that much of the work of teachers is concerned with helping children to read, use and enjoy books, to write effectively and imaginatively, and to appreciate mathematical ideas while utilising these ideas to solve problems.

These skills are more important than geography. Fortunately such a question as to whether children are better engaged in the study of geography or in, say, the writing of a composition, is a false dichotomy. Both goals can be achieved, for geography and the basic skills are closely linked provided that geography is taught with an appreciation of both the breadth of the subject and the needs of children.

This is not to say that other skills are not involved. Clearly skills of hand and eye are closely linked with such aspects of geography as map making, while some of the links between geography and science have been outlined in earlier chapters. Here, however, we are concerned with the basic general skills.

Where reading is concerned the most familiar geography books are still, very probably, the text book series, usually produced in sets of four to cover the four years of the junior stage.

This statement is made despite the claim of a survey carried out by H.M. Inspectorate that only a small percentage of schools—19 per cent—use such books. This does not accord with recent recorded sales of such text books. Certainly such books are often spoken of scornfully by educationists, sometimes on grounds that are not entirely justified. Basically the objections that are raised fall under three headings. The chief objection is that the use of such a set text is conducive to work of a kind that is too dominated by the teacher. Whether this is justified is a matter of debate. Where a class is over-directed it might be more justifiable if the blame were put upon the sheer size of the class or upon the personality and training of the teacher. A lesson can well be centred on a text, yet leave ample choice and scope for children to bring imagination into play and be conducted in a relaxed and pleasantly informal manner. Equally a lesson can appear to be based on modern methods with the children engaged in a wide variety of activities and yet be conducted in an authoritarian fashion. The pattern of a lesson and the degree of formality involved are two totally different aspects.

There is the objection that text books do not link sufficiently closely with the immediate environment. Here there is a measure of truth in the accusation, largely because of the limitations of any school book. Environments vary very widely. Within this country some children are thoroughly familiar with a Cotswold valley, others are at home in a London street. It is clearly impossible for any text book writer to produce a book that is ideally suited to both environments, and any publisher will be quick to point out that a book written solely for the children of a single London district, let alone a single Cotswold valley, would have too limited a circulation to be economic.

Finally there is the objection that any one book purporting to contain a year's work must of necessity deal with material in a very sketchy fashion. Possibly this again is true, for obviously a book must not be forbiddingly thick or prohibitively expensive. However there is no reason why the central text cannot be supported by other books.

Probably the strongest argument that can be offered for text books of this kind is that they offer specialist guidance to the teacher while leaving him the freedom to adjust the material to the needs of a particular class. The widening of the curriculum for younger children with the introduction of new fields (experimental science and French may be instanced) has had the effect of throwing a tremendous burden on teachers. Any teacher, however talented, may reasonably seek help in at least some aspects of the work. Viewed in this way the standard text book becomes rather more a general reference book.

Over the last twenty years a very large number of booklets on geographical themes have appeared. These have the merit of being relatively short (twenty-four to thirty-two pages is usual) so that a child who still has some difficulty over the mechanics of reading can expect to finish one in a short space of time. They also have the merit, since they deal with one single topic only in each booklet, of being able to give a considerable amount of detail.

This matter of detail is important, both in encouraging a child to read and in giving geographical background. Thus while a standard text may not be able to say more than that rice is a staple food in Japan, a booklet dealing with, say, a Japanese family can give much more. A child is often curious to know exactly what rice looks like when it is growing, how the woman of the house prepares rice for a meal, and what the meal is like. 'Are there knives and forks?' 'Do they spread a tablecloth as we do?' These, and a dozen similar queries, are the questions that children ask. Detail of this seemingly trivial nature is important if a sense of reality is to be built up in the child's mind. An analogy can be made here between detail of this kind and the sort of detail a child knows about his father's work. Very many children have never seen their fathers at the place of work, and few fathers have ever sat down and given their children a talk on what exactly the work involves. Yet children frequently have a very clear image of what is entailed. This has been built up from scraps of information, anecdote, and even gossip gleaned from family chatter: that is an image of some clarity has been built up from seemingly trivial detail.

Geography, particularly when the subject is taught by setting specific problems for the children to solve, offers many opportunities for practice in the use of reference books. This is a different skill from the ordinary skill of reading, but one that all educated people require. It is something that can only be developed by constant practice. It is also a skill which develops most readily when work of carefully graded standards of difficulty is introduced. At first, with very young children, it may be merely a matter of a child who is drawing a picture being given a book, shown a photograph in the book, and helped to use the photograph to complete his drawing. This is a very simple operation. Reading does not occur at all: indeed the whole situation hardly deserves consideration in a passage dealing with the use of reference books. Yet this little incident may be of importance to the child, since it is by such seemingly elementary steps that an attitude to reference books is formed.

At a later stage the child may be able to read text sufficiently fluently to derive information from a printed page, but may still need not only the title of the book in which the information is to be found but also the page reference.

Then, as children's skill in handling books increases, they can learn how to use the contents page, and, as the next stage, the index. Step by step they learn how to select the books likely to hold the information that they require. Finally, towards the end of the junior stage, able children are capable of consulting two or even three books, and of combining the information thus taken from more than one source to solve a problem.

Reading can take another form; that of reading a book for enjoyment. One aim of primary education is to bring children to the stage where they will read for pleasure. Geography can be invoked here since many stories have a sound geographical background, and we would wish children to read such stories as much for the background information they contain as for the experience of reading for pleasure. Some geographical literature has a further advantage. Although generalisations are dangerous, it is possible to assert that many boys prefer factual reading material to pure narrative. Certainly many boys in the upper junior school enjoy such books as those of Gerald Durrell, David Attenborough and Jacques Cousteau. They also enjoy books on epic travel such as the children's version of the ascent of Everest and Heyerdahl's account of the Kon Tiki voyage. The appeal of such books is not solely to boys however, as the popularity with girls of Joy Adamson's *Born Free* shows.

Written work, the second general skill to be considered, is, in its many aspects, a key activity in all schools for younger children. This is true to the point where any teacher whose class leaves the primary stage able to write clearly, imaginatively, and with a reasonable minimum of errors may very justifiably feel that the task has been well done. Geography, which by the derivation of the word means 'writing about the earth', provides ample material for purposeful writing activities with younger children. Indeed it offers so many opportunities for written work that it can be used to effect a marked improvement in this general skill in many classes.

It is, of course, quite true that a high proportion of the written work required by the study of geography is purely descriptive. A simple piece of investigation into the nature of some element of the environment demands a record, but such a record makes claim to be no more than a clear and logically stated account of what was seen and what was done. Now much has been done in recent years in revising primary school written work in terms of 'creative writing'; so much that it might seem that there is a division between the aims of language teaching and the aims of geography. Two points would be argued here. First, the value of the ability to produce a clear and logical written record is high, even if such an account lacks imagination or creative thought. Secondly the division between what can be practised in geography and what can be hoped for in creative writing is more apparent in theory than real in classroom practice. Geography includes a wealth of material that is sufficiently exciting to awaken children's interest and to encourage them to write. The story of Scott of the Antarctic or an account of the lunar expedition of Armstrong, Aldrin and Collins both contain enough dramatic elements to catch the imagination of young children.

Similarly the situation of a cargo vessel battling against a gale in the North Atlantic can be presented to children, given only a moderate degree of ability as a story teller on the part of the teacher, as an exciting and stimulating account that children will be ready to emulate. At the time when it took place, the adventure of Captain Kurt Carlsen and his ship the *Flying Enterprise* fascinated young children: such stories are still valid elements in geography teaching.

Clear accounts, whether purely descriptive or imaginative, depend on the ability to construct sentences and to use a good vocabulary forcibly and accurately. Much of the work undertaken with younger children is aimed at developing these abilities. To limit such work to language periods alone is pointless: indeed children can well learn to handle language at the same time as they are increasing their grasp of geographical material.

Within primary schools, mathematics, the successor to the 'rithmetic of the three R's, may well be considered as a tool by which problems can be solved or as a language in which relationships can be stated with precision. Certainly mathematical skills may well be regarded as a general skill that children should master.

Geography has a particular place here in that while it involves a great deal of material likely to fire the imagination of young children, it also entails a high degree of precise measurement. The measurement of quantities in all forms and the handling of the results of measurement are inherent in the study of geography. It must be stressed that geography in its full modern development is implied here. What has been said certainly does not apply to the traditional folk-lore and travellers' tales presentation of igloo-building Eskimoes and Dutchmen in baggy trousers. It does apply where geography involves the use of maps and models, detailed records of the world outside the classroom, precise observations of weather and processes, and accurate studies of more distant places.

No claim is made here that geography is unique. Clearly measurement is also a vital part of science as it is presented to younger children, and science also includes material calculated to hold the interest and attention of young children. Despite this, the existence of a special link between geography and mathematics may still be maintained in discussion.

Geographical studies give ample opportunity for younger children to apply those mathematical skills that are so basic to a full education as to be truly general skills. This is true whether the form of the mathematics in a school is 'modern' or 'traditional'. In the case of traditional mathematics perhaps it is enough to cite a few examples. Thus even with very young children any work on the local shopping centre will involve number. Very early in any investigation children may make will come the queries as to how many shops there are, or the queries concerning the number that sell food or clothing. This same point is made in the official publication *New Thinking in School Geography* (D.E.S. Pamphlet no. 59). This points out that 'as children gain precision they learn to be more precise. "Our road has a lot of traffic" is later more precisely stated as "in half-an-hour we counted 47 cars, 18 lorries, 6 buses, 9 vans, 4 tankers, 8 motorcycles and 22 bicycles passing the school gate" '. There is a direct relationship between this very simple use of number and the elementary statistical techniques that children will begin to encounter much later as they pass into the middle school or secondary school.

Similarly the whole topic of scales involves a direct relationship with mathematics. Taking one activity alone, children in the upper classes of a junior school might well study some plans of houses, and then undertake the more imaginative exercise of drawing a plan of their ideal house. Once this work is started, mathematical skills will come into play. If a child decides that his ideal house should include a really big room for a Scalex car track, then how big is a really big room? Is a room that is four metres square big by domestic standards? What are the measurements of some existing rooms known to the child? An exact figure will be needed if the room is to be drawn to scale on a plan. Then the room will need a door—but how wide is a normal door? Tackling such problems a child gains a real appreciation of what such measurements of length mean in reality, and it can certainly be regarded as a general skill to be able to judge such measurements.

Many other links between the more traditional forms of mathematics taught to younger children and geography will suggest themselves readily to teachers. Others are a little less clear at first sight. Thus the size of warm-blooded animals in cold countries links with area and volume. In the case of any solid, as it increases in size, the volume increases more rapidly than the surface area. Upper juniors can handle the material set out below.

Thus with a cube:

length of side (units)	surface area (square units)	volume (cubic units)	ratio (volume: surface area)
1	6	1	1:6
2	24	8	1:3
3	54	27	1:2

In warm-bloodied animals the rate at which body heat is lost depends on the size of the surface area of the animal. This is a greater problem for animals living in a cold climate than it is for animals that live in a warm area. A bear in the Arctic has a large volume producing heat and a small surface area (compared to its volume) losing it. A mouse has only a small volume producing heat and a comparatively large surface losing it. This is why mice and other small animals cannot face the Arctic winter, and why animals in the far north tend to be larger than related species nearer the equator.

Links with 'modern' mathematics are perhaps a little less well-established if only because such material is still new to many schools and teaching staffs are only beginning to explore its possibilities in relation to the education of young children. Indeed a full treatment of the relevance of geography to some of this material cannot be undertaken yet since we do not know enough about the reaction of children to such studies. However some of the ways in which the newer mathematical concepts and skills can link with geography may be illustrated by specific examples. It is, for instance, now no longer uncommon to find children in the upper reaches of a primary school making a beginning in the study of sets. One necessity is for the teacher to give a wealth of examples so that the children have sufficient practice in this new skill to be able to handle the ideas with confidence. It is here that a link with geography can be made. The relationship between those towns in Britain that have a lot of industry, and those towns that are largely residential with only a little industry, as compared with the towns of Britain as a whole is something that can be most easily expressed in terms of set terminology. Similarly the relationship between desert areas and the land areas of the world as a whole is something most easily shown in a Venn diagram.

To take another topic that is now frequently introduced in the upper classes of primary schools, Cartesian coordinates require similar practice if they are to become really familiar to children. Again what is frequently missed is that this formidable sounding aspect of the 'new' mathematics is represented in the familiar reference system used in such things as the A-Z Street Atlas of Greater London, something that many nine-year olds can handle quite capably. Indeed the use of coordinates can be approached through geographical techniques rather more effectively than through the more usual approach of finding the position of a single desk in a classroom. If a simple street map of the local area is drawn on the playground surface (or on several large sheets of paper pinned to the classroom floor) children will very happily supply Dinky or Matchbox cars so that they can play police car games. The need for a grid reference system can be suggested quite early, and the game allowed to proceed to the point where the 'controller' is ordering his cars to square A3 or square B4, etc.

Finally the close relationship between 'modern' mathematics and geography can perhaps be expressed most easily by reference to a mathematical problem: a genuine problem that exercises adult mathematicians, not one devised for children, even though children find it interesting to seek for a solution.

This is the four-colour map problem. Suppose we take a map of a country, real or imaginary, and divide it up into counties.

We want to colour the map so that counties that have a common border are coloured differently—just as they are in most atlases. How many different colours are needed?

So far no map has ever been drawn that needs more than four colours, although mathematicians and children have tried many times.

8

Records and experiences outside the classroom

Nearly a generation ago a committee of the Royal Geographical Society examined the place of geography in education and came to the conclusion that the inclusion of the subject in the curriculum could be justified in terms of content alone. It was claimed that the facts handled were 'contemporary and real' and that geography was 'significant to every individual and every community'. These comments are still valid, despite the changes in geography and despite the trend towards absorbing geography into a wider field of environmental studies. The stress on the reality of the material to be studied is especially relevant when younger children are concerned.

With very young children the division between fact and fiction is often shadowy to say the least. The legends of the Greek heroes, King Alfred's cakes, the daily life of pygmies in the Congo, and indeed the sagas of television cowboys are all accepted at very much the same level. These are the things that they hear about. All of this is taken in, but at a very different level from the day to day realities of the family, the home, and the local streets. One great value of geographical work is that it helps children to sift their ideas, separating legend from fact, the past from the present, the real from the imaginary.

In attempting to bring home to children the reality of the material that is to be studied the importance of direct experience is clear. This can be illustrated quite dramatically from the responses of older children. For example it is sometimes revealing to ask older town-dwelling pupils, say youngsters about to take O-level, to make a mark on a wall representing the height of a fully grown dairy cow. If the youngsters do this independently so that they are not affected by each other's attempts, a quite astonishing range of answers often results. It is not unreasonable to suggest that there is something amiss if youngsters who can write quite convincingly in an examination about the dairy industry of Somerset cannot indicate the size of the animals concerned, nor is it so unreasonable to regret that they have, apparently, never visited a farm or looked closely at a cow.

Unfortunately work outside the classroom, with younger children at least, is fraught with difficulties. Control becomes more difficult: indeed any teacher who cannot claim to have full control over the children concerned would be well advised to stay within the classroom until this is achieved. Then there is the question of cost, where transport is involved. No school fund is limitless, and parents may be unable or unwilling to contribute. Much more serious is the question of danger, particularly in areas of busy traffic. It may be reasonable to allow fifteen-year olds to work individually or in small groups carrying out simple field work, but, on safety grounds, this can only be justified under very special circumstances with younger children. This safety factor is widely recognised by local education authorities. There are usually regulations stipulating the ratio of responsible adults to children. Clearly the regulations are justified, but, in smaller schools particularly, it does impose problems of organisation as far as staffing is concerned.

As with most difficulties in education, alternative approaches are however possible. Indeed a surprising amount of valuable work can be done without ever leaving the school premises. Weather study is an obvious field here, where most of the work can be done in the school grounds, incidentally avoiding the absurdity that used to be found not infrequently of children studying weather solely by staring at the blackboard and the teacher rather than by looking out of the window at the real thing. At other times much can be done following the 'I Spy' techniques pioneered by the News Chronicle booklets: asking children to make observations on their journeys to and from school and on shopping expeditions with their mothers, and then reporting back in subsequent lessons. To take an example of this, a teacher might decide to base some work on water supplies. A logical starting point lies in the children's own homes, and the majority of children will be familiar with the idea of a storage cistern in the roof. They will know that when water is drawn the cistern can be heard filling for a short while after the tap is turned off. They will be able, in many cases, to describe the cistern, telling of instances when fathers have had to carry out repairs. Further, many will know of a stop cock just inside the garden gate where the main enters the house and will be ready to volunteer information about it. The teacher will want the children to trace the water supply further back, however, back to the water mains in the streets in the first instance. This is where the children can be told of the hydrant signs: usually a black H on a yellow ground, with two numbers fitted into the arms of the H, the upper giving the diameter of the main in inches, the lower giving the distance from the sign to the main in feet. These signs may or may not be familiar, but children can apply the 'I Spy' technique, look for the signs out of school time, and report back. From their reports the pattern of the water mains can be traced— and, of course, the account taken on to its logical conclusion of the source of the water in the mains.

The world outside the classroom is very complex indeed. To study this effectively children need a clear-cut aim. They also need an activity that they can understand, undertake, and complete. The vague and often totally unprepared 'nature walks' that were very fashionable at one time, where children drifted aimlessly behind a teacher who dropped a few facts here and there, with little correlation between these facts, had only limited educational value. Fortunately, within geography, there is such a wide range of techniques of recording information that any child can be given a purposeful task, irrespective of age or ability.

Chief of these methods of recording information is the use of maps. These are the maps indicated as 'maps with records' in the model shown by figure 3 on page 48. These are maps showing a special piece of information gathered by the children themselves and recorded by them. An example of this might be a map of the local shopping centre, where this is neither too large nor too complicated. The children can start with a simple sketch plan, drawn themselves but with, of course, a considerable amount of help from the teacher. The next task is to record what the shops sell by making a list. This information is then transferred to the map, perhaps by encouraging children to suggest pictorial symbols for themselves—a little drawing of a chop for a butcher's shop and so on.

With a typical modern block of some twenty shops, the first impression is of a wide variety of kinds of shop. However this can well be analysed by the children, under guidance from the teacher, and some form of classification introduced. Colours can be put on the maps, over the symbols already used, with all food shops coloured red, all clothing shops coloured green, and so on. The children will soon see for themselves that most shops in a residential area sell things for people's homes, people's stomachs or people's backs.

Towards the upper part of the junior school similar but rather more advanced work can be undertaken. The children of an urban school can study the town centre and thus discover the true function of such a centre. What is to be found in the town centre? Shops certainly, and possibly a market. Shop-keepers and traders need somewhere safe to keep their money, and so there are banks. They also need some means of sending for more goods, and so the main post office is usually in the town centre. But no shopping centre could exist unless there was some way for people to reach it. Where do the bus routes lie? Is there a railway station? Have car parks been provided? Finally trade is not the sole function of a town centre. Is there a church in the centre? Are there cafés, cinemas and parks? Is there a town hall—and what happens in the town hall?

This indicates very briefly the type of work that can be undertaken and the sort of questions that children can meet. There is plenty of material here for study, and it is nearly all material that can be recorded on a map. The Ordnance Survey 50″ to one mile or the 25″ to one mile series would serve admirably here, with the main features of the town centre marked by tiny flags made by gumming coloured paper round pins.

Even more ambitious mapping can be undertaken with able children about to leave the primary stage. For such children what is really land use mapping is possible. Eleven-year olds, unless they are living in a specially complex area, can recognise the difference between residential and industrial areas. They can collect this information the more easily since many eleven-year olds are mobile at least to the point of owning bicycles or being allowed to use buses unaccompanied. Once the information is to hand the children can shade the different areas on a simple street plan of the district. They can also identify and map places that would be of special interest to a visitor, and even undertake, as a project, the compilation of a local guide book.

This is quite advanced work. With younger children similar experience in land use mapping can be attempted for much simpler areas. A town park is often ideal, since there is a much greater measure of safety for the children within its boundaries. Such work might begin with a discussion of what the park contains. Typically there might be a playground area with swings and a slide, an area of carefully tended flower beds, an open area of grass for ball games, a space set aside for tennis or bowls, a paved area for people to stroll with shelters for bad weather, an area set aside for the park-keeper, and so on. All these can be listed, identified and mapped. The results of this work lie in the children gaining mapping skills and a greater understanding of the needs of the community.

'Strip maps', showing a route—that is maps similar to those issued by the Automobile Association—are also a means of recording information that lies within the range of younger children. In a very simple case this might be no more than a representation of the route that children take on their way to school. In at least one school known to the writer, a school set in a post-war housing estate where all the children walk to school and where no very great distances are involved, classes have been asked to add to this by counting the number of steps taken on the journey. The children were later able to convert their paces into metres by pacing a measured length in the playground. Thus the children were able to add the ideas of distance and scale to their maps. Further work included the drawing of simple graphs and finding the average length of journey. In this way the work benefited both their geography and their mathematics.

Mathematical records are, in fact, often very helpful when children study the world that lies immediately beyond the classroom. The very simplest forms are suited to the needs of the youngest children. An example can be instanced here of a teacher seizing an opportunity as it was offered. The school—now happily replaced—was an old nineteenth-century building, set so close to the railway line, raised on a viaduct to a point level with the classroom windows, that conversation was forced to stop when trains went by. The teacher, with a class of infants, not only talked about railways to the children, but went on to link this with the children's work in number. When a goods train went by the teacher and the class carefully counted the waggons, and carried out surprisingly involved calculations about the longest trains seen each day.

This represents a school situation that is, fortunately, rare. Much more common is the circumstance where the school is faced by a line of nineteenth-century terraced houses, all of uniform sizes. These can be counted, and a map drawn to show how they are arranged. Then one house can be selected at random and its frontage measured. The children can then calculate the length of the block and devise a simple linear scale for their map. Possible additional work might involve calculations about the distances such people as postmen, milkmen, etc., have to walk when making their rounds.

Records of traffic are particularly suitable in many areas. Indeed, for many primary schools, the most striking feature of the immediate environment is a major road that runs close to the school building. The idea that a traffic census might be undertaken has already been mentioned (Chapter 6). This is a case where mathematical techniques of recording are suitable, with the children using their observations to construct simple graphs, block diagrams or diagrams of the Isotype nature. Such a traffic census will inevitably be carried out in school hours. However it prompts the query as to whether the road is always as busy. Here the information cannot be obtained by direct observation on the part of the class, but the children can find out from parents or indeed by their own observation outside school hours. The study of traffic on, say, one of the main roads into London, yields an interesting pattern. There is, first of all, the 'rush hour' peak in the early morning. Most of this is passenger traffic; buses and cars, with many of the cars empty except for the driver. Comparable to this is the second 'rush hour' in the evening with the flood of traffic out of the London area. Between these peaks the traffic changes. Depending on the area, the middle of the day sees far more in the way of delivery vehicles and of women drivers heading for the shopping centres. The evening, by comparison, is quieter, with a much higher proportion of heavy long-distance lorries. There is thus a daily rhythm that can be recorded, possibly by a frieze showing traffic at different times of the day. There is certainly a great deal that younger children can learn of the life of the district by studying this rhythm.

Mathematical techniques can be used very effectively where a teacher begins to introduce elements of the physical landscape. Slopes are a case in point. Children use phrases such as 'steep slope' or 'gentle slope' quite indiscriminately until they have studied actual examples in the field. The nature of a piece of rolling ground can be brought home to children quite simply. Let them stretch out an arm at right angles to the body, and then look along the arm towards the spot to which the fingers are pointing. If they then swing round, slowly, keeping the position of the arm locked, their pointing fingers will trace what are really contour lines—even though the term will not be introduced at this stage.

Then the first elements of the measurements of slopes can be started. If one child stands as before, looking along his arm towards the ground, a second child can walk up the slope, counting the paces as he does so, until his feet appear level with the first child's fingers. Different slopes will, of course, require different numbers of paces. It is perhaps worth stressing that at this stage there is no mention of gradients, although these are, in fact, what are being measured. It is enough with young children to note that 'On a gentle slope Jane had to take 16 paces'. 'On the steep slope she took 9 paces.'

In heavily built-up areas, the nature of a slope is often shown, not so much by the ground where it is masked by the camber of roads and the kerbs of pavements, but by the buildings themselves. Thus where a line of terraced houses runs up a slope, each house can be seen to be a brick or two higher than its neighbour. This again can be used to indicate the angle of the slope.

Precisely what can be done in the study of the physical landscape in the immediate environment depends very considerably on the nature of the area. Wherever it is possible to study a small stream a very great deal of extremely valuable work can be done. As before it is very desirable for the children to be given specific problems to solve and to have some specific method of recording the information that they collect. In the case of a small stream a single meander can be examined and a diagram built up showing at which points the banks are steepest, where shallows and beds of pebbles occur, where the water is deepest and where eddies show that the current runs most swiftly. Paper markers, dropped into the stream, will show the way in which the current swings from side to side at a meander, and this too can be added to the diagram.

Even simple pictures can prove a helpful method of recording what is studied outside the classroom. The Plowden Report, quoted earlier in this book (p.12), tells of a walk out of doors being recorded by infants on a large wall frieze. With slightly older children in the lower junior school pictures can be more precise and can show more exact information by being labelled. Thus a building can be studied and a careful drawing made of its façade, noting the various materials used in its construction and the ways in which the materials are used. Bricks, taking a common example, are arranged in a variety of ways according to whether they are forming a load-bearing wall, screening a gap, or bridging doorways and windows. Points like this can be recorded carefully, then studied further when the children have returned to the classroom.

All teachers of young children will be familiar with the way in which youngsters come up with scraps of news. This tendency can be utilised as a form of written record. A class newspaper: a collection of stories, pictures, poems, and jokes, written out by the children and mounted on sheets of sugar paper, is a familiar feature in many classrooms. This can be extended to include local news, by analogy with the local newspaper. Much of the news that children submit is trivial, although this does not mean that talking about it and encouraging children to write it out is a trivial activity. Further, in the hands of an experienced teacher, many of even the more trivial scraps of news can be linked with the geography of the locality. The news that a store has started to dress its windows for Christmas can be turned to the realisation that shop windows reflect the rhythm of the seasons as surely as do the trees in the park. The news that workmen are digging up the road in the High Street leads to the question of what lies beneath the road surface.

Often such items brought in by the children lead to the even more important form of recording where a diary of continuous observation can be maintained. This is particularly the case where a new road or a new building is being erected within reasonable distance of the school.

So far nearly everything that has been said in this chapter about work outside the classroom has been limited to what can be experienced in the immediate vicinity. Matters of finance and time make it inevitable that most of the work will be very local. Nevertheless longer trips are taken with younger children, right up to the most ambitious schemes where upper juniors spend a week or more in a school camp or even on a school journey to a foreign country. These very much more ambitious schemes are sufficiently exceptional to be dismissed here very briefly, but it can be stressed how effective it is from the point of view of the children's geographical experience to let them study an environment that is totally different from their own. Completely rural surroundings, characteristic of many school camp areas, bring home to children exactly how artificial urban conditions really are.

Setting these very long school journeys aside, there are nevertheless a large number of schools for younger children that run full and comprehensive systems of day visits. Many of these expeditions are not geographical in scope, but what can often be done, by a teacher wishing to extract the full value from such trips, is to include some geographical material. A class may be visiting an abbey, but a short detour can bring in a visit to a river as well. Similarly on a visit to Whipsnade, to take a specific example, it is well worth while spending a few minutes drawing benefit from the view from the Chiltern crest.

Other journeys are much more geographical in nature. In many schools this part of the work involves visits to local factories or farms. It is difficult to over-estimate the educational value of such experience outside the classroom, particularly when the visit has been carefully prepared so that every child knows exactly what to look for, and when the visit is followed up by discussions, the writing of records, the construction of maps and diagrams, and some purposeful additional reading.

9
Aspects of activity methods

There is a large and very comprehensive literature on the subject of activity methods and the application of these methods to the education of young children. Further the whole topic is covered exhaustively in any teacher training course or refresher course. However much of this material deals with activity methods in general. The task here is somewhat more limited: this chapter seeks merely to discuss aspects of activity methods as they apply to the teaching of geography and the problems of organising such work with younger children.

Probably the simplest form of activity that can be introduced into a lesson is that of setting children to draw and colour a picture: to discuss a topic for the first part of the lesson then set the children to work illustrating it. As a pattern for a lesson this is certainly not very original, although whether it is quite so poor as to deserve the stigma 'the last resort of the tired teacher' could be argued. Nevertheless it is interesting to take this very simple example to see what children can gain from it. Undoubtedly young children gain experience of hand and eye by practising their skills with paint, crayons or pastels. If left to work alone they gain independence in their arrangement of the pictures and in their choice of colours. But these are general benefits that will be gained whatever the subject. Since our concern here is with geography these can be set aside. More directly it can be argued that by spending some ten or fifteen minutes producing a picture of a topic that is of value to their geographical education children are helped to concentrate on the topic: that by doing this the topic will be fixed more clearly in their minds. This may very possibly be true: certainly it would be difficult to measure even by controlled experiment. However it is the case that with some children at least the picture rather than the topic becomes dominant in their minds as is evident by the way in which they add extraneous details—carefully drawn aircraft passing over what is really a picture of the local shopping centre or even guns added to what is supposed to be a trawler.

Generally the real value of pictures drawn under such circumstances is diagnostic. Indeed for younger children drawing a picture serves as a diagnostic test: the drawing reveals misconceptions in a way that oral questioning does not. Thus a child who shows a dairy farmer taking away a single small churn as a result of milking his herd shows, quite clearly, little idea of the scale of most dairy farms. To have questioned the same child in terms of lorry-loads of churns or of gallons would be far less revealing since, in all likelihood, the child would have little understanding of the terms. If children's drawings are accepted as diagnostic, then they are helpful to the teacher. Just as examining the written work of children enables a teacher to see where a group of children share a common weakness that can then be dealt with, so examining pictures enables a teacher to plan further geographical work. In the case of children wildly underestimating the amount of milk obtained from a dairy herd—to take the example quoted—it might be judged helpful, in a subsequent lesson, to find out the total amount of milk taken daily by all the families represented in the room and then, with the help of reference books, to find whether this involves the yield from one cow or twenty cows.

But the diagnosis of difficulties, though clearly important, is only an initial step in education. Returning to the argument that the value of setting children to draw a picture lies in the fact of their concentrating on the topic, it follows that this concentration is likely to give the most effective results when the children have ample material on which to concentrate. The problem some children are asked to face can be illustrated by analogy. A few years ago an extremely gifted art teacher in a London evening institute used to set new classes of adult students the task of drawing a London bus from memory. He would explain that he was, at that time at least, more concerned with accuracy than with technical skill, and ask his students to be careful to show the bus with

When children are set to draw pictures they can be led away from the theme by their own interests. This boy has drawn a trawler with some high degree of accuracy and has then, left to his own devices for some time, embellished it with guns and aircraft as his attention wandered and he became engrossed in his own imaginings.

the right number of windows along the side, etc. It is worth recording that most of his students found this a very difficult exercise. The teacher then explained his point: that any artists worthy of the name observe accurately. For our purpose here it is worth noting that these adult students—who can be presumed to have more than the average interest in visual matters since they were attending an art class—found difficulty in picturing a familiar object such as a bus with any real accuracy. Children drawing pictures in school are often in a much more difficult position: they are frequently required to draw pictures of something that they have seldom if ever seen.

From this it follows that children set to draw a picture will themselves require plenty of good pictures and need to be helped to use this material in order to achieve accuracy in their work. Thus before attempting to draw a typical cargo boat, a child not only needs to see good, clear pictures of such vessels, but also needs to have attention drawn to such details as the number of funnels such a ship will have.

Even so, as a piece of work this may be stigmatised as being somewhat mechanical. It is perhaps rather sounder, educationally, to suggest a picture that poses rather more of a problem. Possibly children, having seen pictures of a Welsh sheep farm in summer, might be asked to draw pictures to show what it might be like in the depth of winter. A valuable little exercise, along the same lines, is to ask children to draw two pictures—one showing the view from their own bedroom window, the other showing the view that they might expect if they had been born on a Welsh sheep farm—or whatever area is being studied. Clearly children can only do this with help: they need help from the teacher and help from pictorial material. However given this help they can deal with the drawing of the picture as a problem and benefit by solving it.

In all that has been said emphasis has been on accuracy. From the geographical point of view a teacher is not concerned with what a child thinks a Welsh hill farm is like (except from a diagnostic viewpoint) but with what such a farm is like in reality.

It is over this point that there sometimes seems to be a division between art teaching and geography teaching. We may ask children, in their art, to paint an imaginary underwater scene or even an imaginary scene on another planet—and encourage children to give rein to their imaginations to paint in splendidly coloured fish with fantastic shapes or gloriously grotesque bug-eyed monsters. Now this is certainly the opposite of what would be encouraged from a geographical point of view. However it is only one aspect of art teaching. There is another aspect—illustrated by the methods of the evening institute teacher mentioned earlier—that involves exactly the same degree of accurate observation as geography requires. Thus young children, asked to paint a picture, invariably colour the sky a bright blue. Both from the artistic and the geographical aspects of their education we would wish them to look at the sky and see how it really appears. Instances of this kind can be multiplied. Clouds in children's paintings are nearly always of the fair-weather cumulus type—and furthermore children's clouds nearly always have the domes typical of such clouds on all sides as if the cloud were expanding in all directions, downwards as well as up. It takes time, skill and patience on the part of a teacher to help a child to realise that clouds are flat at the base—a realisation that is as much weather study as art. Trees, similarly, in children's pictures, are often of the 'dish mop' form and are usually painted with bright green leaves and rich brown trunks. A good deal of local study must combine with careful art teaching before children really observe what is there.

A much more ambitious aspect of activity methods is involved when models are made—using the word 'model' here in the traditional sense, not in the more recently introduced mathematical sense.

Even the most cursory inspection of children's toys reveals what a large proportion are in fact models. Doll's houses, miniature cars, toy trains and toy soldiers all fall into this category. Of the remainder of children's toys very many are the means of making models—plastic construction kits, materials such as Meccano or Lego, paintboxes and fretwork outfits. The interest of children in models is deep: it develops early and persists, in some cases at least, right into adult life. Why this interest is so intense is not easy to explain: indeed a full explanation would probably involve an analysis of the imitative behaviour of children, and, as with maps, a consideration of the fascination of controlling one's own miniature world. Certainly dramatic play enters largely into children's behaviour as can be seen by watching a small boy playing with a toy car. He will hold it, making it turn and wheel, supplying realistic noises all the while. Clearly he is identifying himself with the driver and with the saga he is enacting in his own mind.

Whatever the root of the delight that children show in models it is clearly sound to use this intense interest as a part of the educational process. Now although models can be used in many fields of study, two aspects of the primary school curriculum lend themselves particularly to model making techniques. These are history and geography.

Taking geography as our particular concern here, one of the aims in teaching this subject is to help children to visualise the lives and surroundings of other people. Lessons on North Sea gas, for example, are designed to build up for the children a mental picture of what it is like to work on a drilling rig well out of sight of land; not an easy thing for children to visualise. If children make a model of a drilling rig they may, in the course of constructing and playing with the model, allow their imaginations full play and identify themselves with the workers on the real rig, much as the small boy, instanced earlier, identified himself with the driver of a car.

A second value of model making with young children is that it ensures that their ideas are precise and detailed. It is quite possible to listen to or to read descriptions, to study pictures and diagrams and to watch film and television presentations, and yet only to have a very vague and superficial idea about the form of a particular object. It is only when children begin to reproduce the object that they realise the need for exact observation and precise detail.

A third value is that if children work together to build up a model which they can exhibit to other classes or which they can display at a parents' evening at the school, they have a tremendous sense of achievement. This is often reflected in their whole attitude to geography and can affect their whole attitude to school.

Despite these values, class models are, unfortunately, one of the most difficult activities to organise. It may be wise for an in-experienced teacher to start with the children making individual models. This can prove a useful piece of work, particularly if precise measurement is involved, thus linking the work with practical arithmetic. But individual model making has the dis-advantage that there is no very obvious use for thirty or more individual models at the end. The best can be exhibited, of course, and the children can take their efforts home to show their parents. Even so, such a lesson tends to end in anti-climax.

It is considerably more satisfactory if the individual models that the children make are such that they can ultimately be grouped together. Thus a model fishing port makes a very satisfactory subject. The children can divide into two groups, making trawlers and buildings respectively. The simplest way of carrying this out is by preparing work cards bearing detailed instructions. The advantage of these prepared instructions lies in the educational value of children learning to follow written instructions and also, at a more utilitarian level, in that the teacher is free to supervise, and not left in the position of having to try to explain work to two groups at once.

While the children are studying their cards, books and pictures in preparation for their work, a few children, probably those with the highest degree of manipulative skills, can be called aside and given instructions about making the base. This small group can add quaysides, and improvise cranes, bollards, etc. Finally, as the other children finish their models, the trawlers and the buildings can be placed in position on the base. Organised in this way, model making does not involve the problems of control inherent when a large number of children are all at work on a single model.

A successful modelling lesson has several requirements. One of the most important is speed. A model that drags on for days or even weeks often not only loses the interest of the children: it

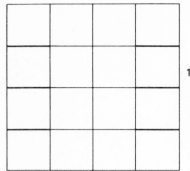

1. Fold a square of paper twice in each direction to make a pattern of 1 6 little squares. Open up the paper and cut along the heavy lines in the diagram

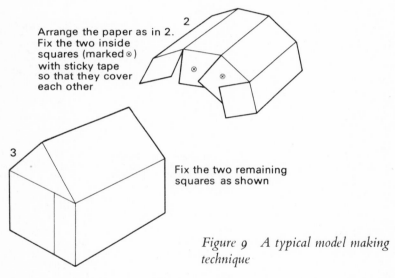

Arrange the paper as in 2. Fix the two inside squares (marked ⊗) with sticky tape so that they cover each other

Fix the two remaining squares as shown

Figure 9   A typical model making technique

becomes a chore. An effective appearance quickly and easily obtained is what is necessary. Over the years teachers have developed a number of very rapid model making techniques suitable for young children. One such technique, which would serve for the buildings of the fishing port described here, is illustrated in figure 9. Since the underlying form of a house is used in a large number of geographical models, this shape, which is well within the capabilities of infants, has a wide application.

A second requirement for a successful model-making lesson is a second activity which the children can take up whenever they have finished their piece of work or whenever they are waiting for help and advice. The great advantage of a second activity, from the teacher's point of view, is that it ensures that all the children have something at hand. Children are always most troublesome when they are idle or bored. This second activity may consist of writing short accounts of the part of the model for which the child is responsible, or it might take the form of the making of a frieze or a set of wall pictures. Either of these pieces of work can be pinned up on the wall behind the model to add interest to the final display.

A very different form of activity is that represented by making collections. There is a squirrel-like tendency in many primary school children: a readiness to make collections of all manner of things from conkers to match-box labels. This is a tendency that teachers have been quick to exploit: it is also something that links easily with geography. Stamps, for instance, offer such a possibility since many pictorial stamps feature maps prominently. In 1966 Sir Dudley Stamp said: 'As a very rough guide I estimate that there are about a thousand map stamps. No great rarities are included so that a complete or almost complete collection is a reasonable proposition—with a vast amount to be learnt from careful study.'

There are other equally relevant articles which can be collected. Under guidance a collection of food labels has a similar value, so have collections of wild flowers in that they give indications of the distributions that are the basis of geographical study. The phrase 'under guidance' is used advisedly here. Making a collection may have an intrinsic value to a child, but the full geographical value of such an activity only comes when a child is guided to see the significance of what he has done. Thus a collection of labels from tins of food becomes much more valuable if it is linked with a map; a collection of rocks more valuable if the specimens are labelled; a collection of stamps if it is accompanied by notes about the countries of origin.

From the aspect of organisation, collecting can be handled in two ways. For many children collecting is an individual, even solitary, activity. A teacher can accept this, merely encouraging the child to talk about his hobby and perhaps encouraging him to display his collection on the class 'interest table'. Alternatively collecting can be organised on a group or even a class basis, as when a number of children are encouraged to collect labels from oranges as one aspect of a topic on fruit.

It has been pointed out that 'learning, the educational process, has long been associated only with the glum. We speak of the "serious" student'. (M. McLuhan, *The Medium is the Message*, 1967.) Whatever general truth we may consider is contained in this, it hardly applies to newer activities developed by teachers of geography. Indeed one of the most recent developments has been in the form of 'geographical games'. These, (as R. Walford, a leading exponent in this field, pointed out in *Geography* 1969) are not 'those of the quiz variety or indeed any of those marginal divertissements which are designed for wet Friday afternoons'. Yet they are true games in the sense in which 'monopoly' is a game or as we speak of 'war games'.

Most of these operational games are really for secondary school pupils. However some are being used in junior schools. Some of these are contained in some recent school text books (Cole and Beynon, *New Ways in Geography*, Basil Blackwell). One additional game, which we may call 'Building a Motorway', can be described here.

The board is prepared by the children themselves (and may be taken home at Christmas as a present for a brother or sister). Basically the board is a sheet of squared paper mounted on card (a pattern of hexagons is better, but this is much more difficult to draw, and paper printed in such a way is not so readily obtainable in schools). The game is played with counters: these need be no more elaborate than small pieces of card. Each player requires a handful of counters: the exact number does not matter.

The object of the game is to build up an unbroken line of counters from any point on the 'Start' line to any point on the

Figure 10   The board prepared for 'Building a Motorway'

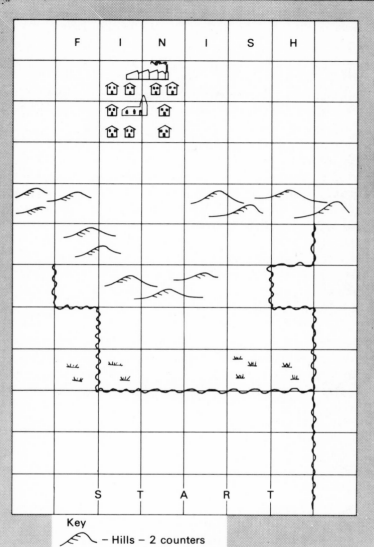

Key

— Hills – 2 counters

— River–4 counters

— Marsh–3 counters

— Town–10 counters

'Finish' line using the least possible number of counters. Players take turns. Counters may be laid on a square next to the one already occupied—working along any rank, file, or diagonal, rather like the movements of a king in chess.

When the children prepare the board they shade in some squares to represent hills, mark others to represent marshes, and add rivers (see figure 10). Some guidance can be given here to make sure that these features are shown in reasonable places: that rivers do not run up hills and so on. In playing, any square that is marked as a hill requires two counters to show the increased cost of making cuttings for the motorway. A marsh requires three counters per square to show the difficulty of embankments, while a river crossing requires four counters to allow for the cost of making a bridge.

Depending on the ability of the class any number of complications may be introduced—parkland or good farming land can be shown as more valuable than the rest for example. Built-up areas may be judged worth ten counters per square.

The point of this game lies in the fact that the children, while designing the board and while playing, are in fact meeting some of the difficulties actually encountered by the designers of motorways. They are, indeed, learning an advanced geographical idea, the idea that land varies in value. Yet it is still play. The experienced teacher will appreciate this play element and know how to gain the maximum value from it.

Part 3

Fields of geography

10

The immediate environment

A fundamental problem that underlies any attempt to prepare a scheme of work for younger children that includes geography is that of achieving a balance between work on the immediate environment and work on more distant places. If a course concentrates solely on the locality it will miss much of the advantage that can be gained from using children's sense of wonder. On the other hand, work on more distant places must rely on such things as pictures, books, films, accounts given by people who have themselves visited the places, samples, models, and similar aids. All these things have undeniable value, but all this must be regarded as second-hand material as far as the children are concerned. Excluding the special case of the school journey, it is only in the case of the immediate environment that a child's experience can be truly direct. This must be set beside what is known of the value of direct experience as far as young children are concerned. Indeed the recognition that the great majority of younger children can only learn efficiently from concrete situations is one of the most important conclusions of the school of research associated particulary with Piaget and also with Baldwin, Isaacs, Luria and Bruner.

An immediate application of this argument leads to the recognition of the idea that what can be learned by children through their senses should be the prelude to that learning which depends heavily on children's imagination and their ability to interpret reports made in various ways by other people. This was pointed out, with special reference to geography and younger children, some forty years ago by Helen Thomas who, dealing with the problems of giving seven-year-olds an idea of tropical climates, wrote:

'Encourage the children to recall the warmest weather they have ever experienced; how they felt, how they dressed, what they did; let them talk freely until they more or less reconstruct in their consciousness the feel of continued humid heat. Help them to imagine what it is like to live in a country where that kind and degree of heat are the rule day in and day out.

'. . . we do well to remind ourselves that while to the adult mind the idea of summer heat continuing throughout the year is utterly simple, a child may read such a statement with a certain degree of mental understanding of the words, and yet have no real consciousness of its concrete meaning. It is not a matter of stupidity on his part, but simply one of lack of experience.' (Helen Thomas, *Teaching Geography*, Ginn and Co.)

Accepting the value of the study of the immediate surroundings, a number of problems emerge. Thus in this branch of study local conditions vary so widely that a teacher cannot rely on guidance from books in the same way that he can with themes that have a wider appeal.

Even the question as to what constitutes the environment is not easily answered. In a simple case the immediate environment can be defined as the area in the vicinity of the home, the school, the church and the shops. It has been suggested that the local area can be delineated by sticking pins in a map to show where the children live, then drawing a rough circle round these pins. However this is only realistic in the very simplest of cases. For many young children the land with which they are thoroughly familiar comes as a set of regions. Thus, as well as the immediate surroundings of the home, children frequently know the town centre very well as a result of shopping expeditions, but are often quite ignorant of the streets between the two zones except in so far as these can be seen through the windows of a bus or a car. Where, as in some London cases, travel to the local main shopping centre involves a short underground journey, the link between the two is even more tenuous. Adding to this difficulty, many children have other areas which, to them, are local. This is the case where regular visits are paid to grandparents who take them for walks in that vicinity. Shown cartographically the 'home ground' of many a five-year-old would appear as a number of separate patches on a map.

At the present one of the greatest problems of education lies in the gulf that frequently exists between educational theory and classroom practice. On one hand are the researches of such scholars as Piaget: writings that are often difficult to understand and indeed almost impossible to express except in technical terms, and which give only general guidance. On the other hand there are the practical difficulties facing the teacher: the problems of organisation resulting from over-large classes and insufficient material resources, and, above all, the problems of selecting suitable objects or themes for study and devising effective activities for the children. The success of those educational journals that attempt to link academic research with professional practice by giving factual advice (*The Teacher's World* is an example) is a measure of the importance of this gulf.

This situation creates the greatest degree of difficulty in those areas that offer the fewest possibilities as far as local geography and local field work are concerned. Such conditions are typical of the suburban margins of big cities and specially characteristic of the fringe of London. It is not easy to draw up a scheme of study directly related to a large zone of the virtually identical semi-detached houses that characterised the '30s, particularly if this building, as was often the case, was allowed to spread across a broad river terrace giving little or no relief features and enabling the builders to obliterate nearly every trace of the previous use of the land. Similarly many big cities have large areas where the only buildings are late nineteenth-century terraced houses of the 'tunnel-back' type, set in a pattern of long straight streets with little to break the monotony. As in the '30s the builders favoured areas with little or no relief, so these aspects of geography cannot be seen either. Since both types of area are almost entirely residential, schools tend to be set in central positions with little in the immediate vicinity of the school to suggest geographical interest. In such areas not even local occupations offer much promise of fruitful study since it is often the case that the majority of the wage-earners commute to places of work set some distance away, and, as is often the case in large cities, these people are engaged in work that is too complex to be studied by young children.

Under such conditions geographical studies tend to fall to a minimum, and where children are taken out of the classroom such expeditions tend to be of longer range, usually directed to visits to zoos, cathedrals, castles and similar places of clear-cut interest.

Nevertheless, despite the intractible nature of the environment, a great deal of geographical work that has real value is still possible. Thus the study of soils is worthy of inclusion in a primary course, if only because, to many urban children, soil is 'just dirt' and not the source of most of our food and clothing.

Detailed scientific work on soils is out of place here, but children can make observations that will prepare them for the more advanced work that they will meet in the secondary stage.

The work that children do can take several forms. A beginning might be made by looking at the pebbles that are to be found in most soils. As a result of the Pleistocene glaciation, many of the soils of Great Britain exhibit a wide variety of pebbles. Thus in north London a few minutes search on a piece of bare ground will yield blue/black flints from the Chilterns, red 'liver' quartzites from the Midlands, pure white quartz fragments and toffee-coloured flints that have been stained with iron. There is, of course, no point in naming these pebbles or in mentioning their place of origin to the children. The children we are considering here are too young for this: it is enough for them at this stage to gain a fresh insight into a seemingly very commonplace aspect of their world.

A collection of pebbles can be made. It will be found that if these are wetted the colour becomes very much more striking. This effect can be made permanent by giving the pebbles a coat of clear varnish. A link with art can be forged here, since the brightly coloured pebbles can be used to make mosaics by mounting them in plaster or plasticene.

Similarly the texture of the soil can be studied. The variety of soils within Britain is so great that even in the small area represented by the catchment area of a primary school considerable variations can be found. Fathers who are keen gardeners will often help children to realise that even the soil in a small suburban garden may vary from one flower bed to the next. A simple experiment will show the difference between, say, clay soils and sandy soils. If samples of the two soils are packed tightly into identical flower pots, children will find that water penetrates at very different rates.

A second example of work that can be undertaken in the least promising of environments concerns the building materials used in the children's homes and the children's school. Mention has already been made of the way in which children can be asked to make sketches to show the way in which bricks are used in building, but such a study, with children in the middle years of the primary school, can go more deeply into this whole topic. The children can be helped to compile a list of all the principal materials that go into the building of a house: bricks, cement, plaster, tiles, wood, metals, etc. Then a number of questions can be considered. How are these materials used? How are they fastened together? Where do the materials come from? At this stage children can begin an investigation, possibly working in groups according to the material of their choice. During this work, because of the nature of the materials, a number of simple experiments are possible, many of which provide links with such fields as science and mathematics. Thus if a brick is placed flat in a dish containing a little water, the water will soak up to the top of the brick. If a second brick is placed on top of the first, the water will continue to climb. How this is prevented can lead to the genuine 'discovery' of the existence of a damp course. (In domestic building this is usually marked by a layer of bituminous material in the brickwork some eighteen inches from ground level.) How this can be reproduced in the class room experiment offers an opportunity for further investigation. The children can be led to find that a layer of impervious kitchen foil will serve.

Similarly a link with the mathematics of shapes can be made when the wooden rafters of a house are considered. In normal domestic building practice wooden rafters are used in threes, set in vertical triangles with two beams forming the sides of the roof and the third beam forming the cross bar. That the third beam does more than merely form the ceiling can be shown by experiment. If two cigarette packets are stood facing each other to form 'walls' and an attempt is made to place an opened book over them to form a 'roof' it will be found that this is impossible. The weight of the book inevitably thrusts the 'walls' over sideways. However if a couple of rulers are added, representing the cross beams of the roof, the book can be placed quite securely, thus demonstrating an aspect of the geometry of triangles.

Thus even the least promising environment can be brought into use in the teaching of geography to younger children. As the Plowden Report points out, on the subject of difficult areas, 'the weather and the stars are available to all'.

Geography is normally considered in terms of the present, but this is not necessarily always the case. Thus there is the academic study known as historical geography: a study the aims of which can be defined as the reconstruction of past geographies. While this is properly an advanced study at university level, some of the ideas can well be applied to work on the immediate environment that young children can comprehend. Thus within the Greater London area there are thirty four road names including Alma— the battle in the Crimean War. There are also seven roads named after Mafeking. The choice of road names can be significant. Mafeking may be taken as an example. Prior to the South African War few people in Britain would have known the name. Quite shortly after the war it dropped from prominence. However it was very much in people's minds for a short while, and builders used it to name streets. Now if a Mafeking Street exists in the vicinity of a school it is interesting to examine it and try to reconstruct what it was like when it was first built. Thus children are often both interested and surprised to find that when the first people moved in to the houses, their furniture would have been brought in horse-drawn waggons. What else would have been different? What was this whole district like when these roads were first laid out? These are all valid lines that a class investigation can follow.

The reconstruction of past geographies is a topic that is particularly useful in an area of older housing such as is suggested by the name Mafeking Road. It is frequently, although not invariably, the case that such an area contains a relatively high proportion of people who have known the area for a long while. Some of the information can come from parents and grandparents, and this enlisting of help from the home, through enquiries made by the children, can strengthen parent—teacher relationships. It is also probable, in such an area, that the local library or the local paper will have records that are made available, possibly in photostat form, for children to study.

Academic geography is also concerned with planning, and this is a second case where advanced studies suggest very suitable work for young children. A situation may well occur where some alteration to the local road system—the introduction of a one-way system or the building of a new road intersection—brings home to the children the idea that conditions are changing. What other changes in the roads could be made with advantage? Alternatively some older houses may be demolished and a new building put in their place: that is the skyline is changing visibly before the children's eyes. It is quite justifiable, within the field of geography, to ask what the locality is going to be like in the year 2000: that is to spend a little time projecting future geographies.

II
Distant environments

Despite all that has been said about the value of studies based on the environment, particularly where such studies involve field work, a course for younger children that was based entirely on such purely local material would be too parochial. Such a course would ignore many of the interests of children, many of whom are deeply concerned about such events as the disastrous fire aboard the Queen Elizabeth in Hong Kong harbour. Such a course would deny children the fascination of distant places: it might well be considered to ignore the maturity reached by older children within the primary stage, and it would certainly fail to take into account the effects of television in the home and the growing tendency to take family holidays in distant environments. Such a course would also rob geography of many of the opportunities of furthering racial understanding, since it is while studying something of southern Asia that a primary child learns that the conical hat of the peasant farmer in the Asian tropics is not 'funny' but a sensible and practical headgear made cheaply from local materials. Finally a purely local course might well be accused of offering too tenuous a link with existing secondary schemes.

On all these counts a convincing case can be argued for a course that contains a measure of study of places that lie beyond the immediate environment.

If this is accepted, the problems facing teachers concern the selection of material and both the manner and timing of its introduction. An analysis of timetables, syllabuses, and children's books of a few years ago shows that at one time geography, as presented to younger children, was broken down into local studies, studies of Great Britain (or the British Isles), and world studies. This three-fold division had the advantage of being logical, clear-cut and sound geographically. Further it allowed for easy syllabus planning within the junior school.

With the youngest children, in recognition of their stage of development, local studies occupied the greatest part of their time, although some work was also done on Britain and some stories at least (e.g. *Rikki-tikki-tavi*) introduced concepts of world geography. The proportion of time allotted to local studies was allowed to decrease as a child passed through the school until it became a relatively small proportion of the work of the fourth year. Meanwhile the work on the geography of Britain was increased until it became dominant in the third year. Indeed a tradition grew up that much of the work of this nine- to ten-year-old age group should be based on the geography of Britain. An argument in favour of this was that by the age of nine many children would have had experience outside their immediate locality and would know at least some towns and villages beyond their area. Thus the division between Britain and their local area became blurred. In the final year, based on the argument that the children had greater ability to deal with the problems of comprehension, world studies took a major place. This was also regarded as helping in the transition from the primary to the secondary stage.

As a pattern this basis for a scheme of work would be regarded as dated by many teachers: nevertheless it is still followed in a number of schools. It certainly possesses considerable advantages, since it does bear a relationship to the observed development of children. At a purely administrative level it is clearcut and allows a syllabus to be formulated in a way that gives precise guidance to the individual teacher—something that is of considerable value in those schools where rapid staff changes occur.

Nevertheless it is advisable to modify such a pattern. To a London child Brighton and Southend may very well be familiar, but Clydebank and the Orkneys will only be known to the occasional child who has an unusual family background. Because of this, it became usual by the early '6os to speak of the child's 'homeland'. Homeland, as a term, is not completely synonymous with Great Britain, although a study of Great Britain embraces the study of the homeland. The idea of studies of the homeland is that the course should be weighted towards the child's native major area. Thus in Welsh schools, for example, the course would be weighted towards Wales, and children in Durham would be more concerned with the northern counties that with those of the south.

This modification is useful, although, obviously, the term homeland lacks geographical precision.

More recently still a further important modification to the original planning scheme has become common. The division between Great Britain or even the less well-defined homeland on one hand and the world beyond on the other is logical to the adult mind. It does not, however, follow the workings of the minds of children. To very many children in Liverpool, Lancaster is as different and distant as Marseilles. The fact that one lies in the same geographical unit while the other does not is not significant to children. For this reason the division between the homeland and the world beyond has become increasingly vague and many teachers, in planning, would place both areas of study under a single heading. Both are concerned with distant environments.

This change is perhaps significant in reflecting a strong general trend towards a curriculum based on the needs of children rather than on the logic of subjects.

Facing the problems of studies beyond the immediate locality in a way more directly related to the immediate problems of lesson planning, the ways in which a particular topic can be handled in the classroom must be considered. This choice of an approach is important, for it is often the way in which material is presented that fires the interest of children. The importance of the impact of a new approach was recalled by Professor Alice Garnett, speaking at the Geographical Association in 1968. She recalled that her own schooldays were largely capes and bays. 'Later however . . . capes and bays were dramatically replaced by "Homes in Many Lands" '—a change that had far reaching influence on her attitudes.

Many teachers have experimented in teaching the geography of distant places to younger children, with the result that a wide and sometimes bewildering variety of approaches have been developed. Despite this, a classification of approaches is possible.

One fundamental development took place when Herbertson first advanced his system of regions. Since then the growth of the idea of a regional approach has affected geography teaching at every level, although geography as taught at the universities is now swinging markedly away from it. Regional geography is especially well established in secondary schools, particularly with the more academically inclined pupils. It must be stressed that the purely regional approach, developed as it was in the grammar schools, is unsuitable for the primary stage. Where it is to be found it can often be traced to a teacher who did little or no geography while at college and who is falling back on what she did herself while at school. Yet one variant of the regional approach did become established, and a number of schools followed a broadly regional pattern with younger juniors, usually studying such topics as 'the hunters of the great white north' or 'pygmies of the great forests'.

Such treatments often resulted in sterotyped figures that had little reality in the minds of children. The approach failed because it was based on a fallacy: it was an attempt to give the general before the specific. Yet it is far too sweeping to dismiss this treatment as devoid of all merit. There is currently a demand from teachers of lower primary classes for short, easy to read booklets that give children an accurate first impression of what deserts, forests and polar areas are like. This demand recognises that, even if the school tends to be strongly oriented towards the study of the immediate environment, children do hear of distant places and want to know more about them.

Another approach that has achieved popularity is the technique of making a comparative study of things that are known to the children and equally well known elsewhere. The 'homes in many lands' theme referred to by Professor Garnett falls into this category. Similar themes include transport or food or clothes in many lands.

The most serious drawback of this approach is the danger that a teacher will, understandably, aim for the sharpest possible contrasts, and in so doing give information that is badly out-of-date. Thus in dealing with 'homes round the world' it is very tempting to include igloos, wigwams and yurts. Although a log cabin makes a striking contrast with the homes with which most of the children will be familiar, it is poor teaching to leave children with the impression that most Canadians live in log cabins. A similar situation occurs with 'transport'. 'Transport in many lands' is probably most truthfully portrayed in terms of the ubiquitous Ford truck: certainly this is a far more common form of transport than camel caravans, llama trains or dog teams. It is interesting to note that when a recent trans-Arctic expedition set out from Alaska using dog teams, the local population turned up, on motorised sledges, to watch this novelty. Many brought their children since the youngsters had never seen dogs used for transport before.

This is not to advise against using such themes as 'homes' or 'transport'. There are many contrasts that have very real geographical significance. Thus many modern school buildings in this country have very large windows to catch as much sun as possible and heating systems to warm the rooms in winter. An equivalent building in, say, Malaysia, would be much more likely to have concrete slabs jutting out on all sides of the windows to shield the glass from the glare of the sun. There would be no heating system, but there would be air-conditioning or at least an electric fan. Similarly, driving across the American desert, with emergency water caches every few miles and with the problem of drifting sand obscuring the road, presents a contrast with anything that children in this country are likely to have met.

Even with food there is the danger of presenting out-of-date material. Gauchoes subsisting almost entirely on meat and sipping maté tea through a straw make a fascinating picture—but not one that can be taken as remotely resembling modern Argentinians. Of course variations in meals can be brought out to reflect geographical conditions. Chinese diets, for example contain little or no dairy products. Chinese restaurants are now sufficiently common for children to check this for themselves. The children can learn that large herds of cattle cannot be maintained under the intensive farming system of the densely peopled areas of China.

This last point can be taken further as a step towards racial understanding. To many Chinese the smell of cheese is distasteful. Indeed, although it would be considered impolite to mention it, they sometimes find Europeans distasteful in that the scent of cheese lingers, rather as North Europeans find the smell of garlic unpleasant on the person of someone who habitually eats it. For children to learn that they may be the ones that are distasteful may help them to form attitudes that are less contemptuous of other races.

This point of racial toleration is one that is closely linked to an approach of this kind. The fact that a modern building in Malaysia would be air-conditioned was mentioned above. Recently the Prime Minister of the neighbouring state of Singapore spoke on television and, during the interview, drew a little verbal picture of a man who was reasonably affluent as 'having a nice house, air conditioning and so on'. An Englishman would have used a similar description but would have said 'central heating'. It is easy to be slightly patronising towards an Asian who lives in a mud hut. True comparisons between equals are far less likely to create this situation.

A third broad classification of approaches is that represented by 'peoples of many lands'. Often this is concerned with children and is presented as 'children of many lands' As such it rests on seemingly unexceptional grounds, based as it is on the idea that children can learn how their daily lives would have differed if they had happened to have been born in another place. The idea that children are interested in other children is fundamental to this approach. It is open to criticism, however, on grounds derived from watching children at play. Young children will play cowboys or soldiers or spacemen, but not cowboys' children, soldiers' children or spacemen's children. Even when children play at schools, it is usually the case that it is the youngest and smallest children who are bullied into taking the part of the class. Further, especially in the more advanced communities, the life of children living in distant areas is too similar to the life of the children themselves to be fruitful of much geographical comparison.

Where 'peoples of many lands' is dealing with adults it can be much more fruitful and less artificial. Problems of selection occur just the same. Which peoples are to be taken as examples to be studied? There is the danger, as with the themes discussed earlier, of selecting people from a very primitive community, or people who are not typical of the area in which they live. This is a problem that can be illustrated most clearly by reversing the process, and asking ourselves, were we teaching in Japan or Peru, what sort of figure we should select to represent Britain in a scheme of work for Japanese or Peruvian children.

A fourth broad group within this classification of approaches is that associated with specific topics. Within this category can be listed all those approaches that involve selecting a food or a material and tracing it to its source. Thus children study 'wheat' or 'wool'. An early example of this was produced by Fairgrieve who wrote of 'the geography of the breakfast table'. Such an approach has certain advantages. By tracing such a food as New Zealand lamb links can be made between the immediate environment and the distant source: the route the meat takes can be traced from the local shop, back to the market, the docks, and then to the ship that brought the meat. Such a treatment can be used, as was suggested earlier, to establish the interdependence of mankind.

With such an approach there is often the strictly utilitarian point that, since most of the materials involved are of commercial value, there are firms involved who are often prepared to supply pictures or even whole study kits.

A further group of approaches is made up of studies in which journeys are considered. These may be real journeys, as when children study Heyerdahl's voyage in the Kon Tiki, or a strong element of imagination may be evoked as when children-study what they might see if they made a journey down the Thames from source to mouth or if they were to fly from Heathrow to New York.

Very much depends here on the quality of the aids available.

A gripping story as in the case of Thor Heyerdahl may bring a lesson to life. Alternatively plenty of striking pictures may make an imaginary voyage very real to young children.

A new criterion for a classification of approaches to world studies is involved when using sample studies as a teaching method, even though these began many years ago. The way in which sample studies differ from more conventional ones can be illustrated from a single book—a book which pioneered this technique. In 1942, Platt, an American geographer, produced a book for adults entitled *Latin America—Countrysides and United Regions.* The book, instead of dealing with the general geography of regions or of countries as was conventional at the time, dealt instead with single units: a single trading post on the River Amazon or a single nitrate plant in the Atacama Desert. There was no attempt to draw generalisations; rather the reader was given a wealth of detail about a single simple unit that was judged to be typical of each area. The technique was taken up for secondary school use, notably by Fairgrieve and Young in a series called *Real Geography,* and, more recently, by Rushby, Dell and Dybeck in the series *Study Geography.*

As a teaching technique sample studies has much to commend it. These studies, based as they are on fact, carry much of the authenticity of local geography and permit genuine comparisons with the home region.

It is also fair to point out that this approach has certain defects. Detailed information about a single village, a single home, a single farm or plantation or indeed a single family, is virtually impossible to obtain without long residence in the country. A teacher living in this country can look up the agricultural statistics of Bolivia without difficulty providing that a good library is available. What is difficult to obtain is information about what a Bolivian family has for breakfast—or indeed, whether Bolivians eat at that time of day at all. Even where a traveller has written a book and made the information available it is difficult for a teacher to judge to what extent the information is truly typical. As earlier, a teacher can place himself in the reverse position. Teaching foreign children he might mention the traditional

English breakfast—but how many English people really eat such a meal at that time of the day?

A curious result of these difficulties is that when sample studies are followed the lesson is more closely tied to the book for information than ever before, because the teacher has no more information about the sample than is presented in the text. Obviously a teacher can use superior skills in interpreting both text and pictures as offered by the book, but this does not alter the position greatly. There are a few exceptions. The Geographical Association have published a booklet containing details of some sample studies in Asia, while the Association of Agriculture have published a whole series of 'farm adoption' folders. In these cases the teacher has more information than will ever be required by the class and thus gains more freedom in lesson planning. However these detailed studies are small in number.

Particular interest currently centres round what are often termed 'problem based' approaches. These frequently centre round such topics as world food supplies (thus Oxfam have produced a work scheme). Much excellent work has been done here, but such a treatment must be introduced with circumspection. Many of the problems that can be handled in such a way involve ideas and moral judgements that are very advanced for all but the most able classes. World food supplies, instanced here, is a case in point. To a young child the whole situation is simple and can be expressed as 'Why don't we send them some of our food?' The scale and nature of the problem is beyond a child's comprehension; he cannot appreciate the financial and technical problems and has no idea of the political difficulties involved. Because of this problem-based teaching is more suitable when linked to the locality, where the realities of the problem are more likely to be appreciated than when linked with distant places.

This synoptic view of approaches in use must, in at least one way, be unsatisfactory. It is not possible to suggest any one technique that is markedly superior to the others. Even if such a decision were possible, it would only express a situation that exists at this moment of time. Thus even where an excellent sample study exists, as in the case of some Indian villages, where conditions might be regarded as relatively static, the material is beginning to date. The motor bus and the transistor radio have made such changes in Indian village life that earlier studies may well be regarded as no longer wholly typical.

A second variable must be added to this. There is sound medical evidence to show that children in primary schools are reaching physical maturity earlier that they did in previous generations. As children mature, their patterns of thought change also—and this must now be allowed for. There is also evidence, backed by the experience of a large number of teachers, that, in the case of urban children at least, there is a greater measure of sophistication than existed earlier. This again affects the presentation of material in a lesson. Black and white television lessons are likely to be regarded somewhat scornfully when there is colour television in the home, and, generally, what was accepted contentedly ten years ago is likely to be dismissed as 'kid's stuff' today.

In studying distant environments the place of such secondary sources of information as films, filmstrips, television and radio must be considered. The value of these can be appreciated if an attempt is made to understand the mind of a child. To an adult, even though no formal studies in geography have been undertaken since childhood, a word such as 'jungle' conjures up a picture: a picture built up over the years by the casual and often unconscious accumulation of information from many sources. Young children are still in the stage of building up this background, and it is in helping this process that films, filmstrips and broadcasts have their greatest value.

Yet these aids have drawbacks. Writing of film, a leading authority has stressed the need for film makers to decide at the initial planning stage exactly the audience for which the film is designed, stating that 'even in the case of films made to instruct, too little thought is sometimes given at the outset as to the probable age-group and mental capacity of those to be instructed, and to how many instructional points can, in fact, be put over effectively in one film.' He concludes that 'it is very seldom possible to produce a successful film for more that one type of audience'. (W. H. Baddeley, *The Technique of Documentary Film Produc-*

tion, Focal Press, 1969.) However commercial firms producing films are also faced with the necessity of selling their products to the widest possible market. The cost of film production makes this inevitable. Because of this it is not unusual for educational films to be recommended somewhat broadly as suitable for upper primary and secondary pupils.

It follows from this that teachers of younger children need to select film with care and to use it rather that merely show it. It is necessary to prepare children for the film by giving them points to look for and problems to solve, to follow up the film with specific questions, and, indeed, be prepared to halt the film during a showing in order to stress a particular point.

Filmstrips fall into a similar pattern. It was pointed out earlier in this book that short filmstrips are not commercially practicable. However few classes can profitably sit through the fifty 'frames' that make up a normal filmstrip. It is necessary for the teacher to select merely those frames which have immediate relevance.

This highlights the fundamental problem of using television and radio with younger children. Excellent though many of these programmes are, they must be used exactly as they are presented. Editing is not possible (except in the limited case of radio lessons pre-recorded on tape). Essentially the teacher must surrender the class to the broadcaster. It follows that the need for work designed with those particular children in mind as a follow-up is even more pressing.

With young children a further difficulty arises from the very nature of the pictures involved in films, filmstrips and television. A camera records everything that is before it, and, although a skilful operator can select a view that forces the chosen subject to the attention of the viewer, there is no guarantee that this will always work with children. It is by no means uncommon, when a group of children are shown a picture, for some of the group to pay more attention to some trivial detail than to the main point. A picture may show the milking parlour on a dairy farm, but to an individual child it may be a picture of a cow with an oddly-shaped horn. This tendency of children to focus on detail is recognised, and indeed the term 'background noise'—an analogy with sound recording—has been used by those concerned with teaching by pictures to describe distracting detail.

Yet despite these strictures that value of such secondary sources must be re-affirmed. They have a real part to play in giving a sense of reality to work on distant environments.

12

Integration and achievement

'Integration' is a word that carries special implications in education. Indeed its use suggests a particular attitude towards teaching and a particular philosophy of education. Yet the precise meaning of the word is singularly ill-defined: it is applied variously to any system that may be claimed to establish the unitary nature of knowledge.

The idea of intergration is by no means new. Even if an examination of educational trends is restricted solely to the period since the ending of the Second World War, the idea of integration in schools can be seen to occur frequently. Geography, as a subject, has been involved in nearly every case, so a consideration of these trends is germane here.

In the immediate post-war years, up to the late '50s, the idea of integration was applied most commonly to history and geography. In many schools attempts were made to link these two subjects into a new discipline of 'social studies'. One reason underlying the introduction of this new study can be appreciated if social studies is regarded as reflecting the intellectual and social climate of the time. The decade following the end of the war was a period of upheaval in society, a period characterised by rapid social change. This was the period that produced the Welfare State. It was, above all, a time of intense interest in society. A second factor working parallel to this general intellectual climate resulted from the composition of the teaching force. Immediately after the war, to make good a serious national shortage of teachers, 'emergency colleges' were set up, giving shortened courses of basic training to people—largely ex-servicemen—whose careers had been interrupted by the war. The teachers seconded from schools to run these courses were just the people who were affected by, and indeed had helped to create, the interest in social change. Similarly many of the mature students, by the nature of their war-time experiences, were ready to question the existing social order. Indeed they were in part prepared for this by the Services. A feature of the war-time Services was an educational programme including 'B.W.P.' ('British Way and Purpose') lectures which were heavily weighted towards social matters. These influences meant that many teachers trained at this time welcomed the new field of social studies.

Despite the initial promise of this attempt at integration, social studies lost impetus and died away, although some of the ideas contained in it had a lasting effect on education. Basically the inherent defect of social studies lay in the difficulty of blending the two disciplines of history and geography. Thus while the changes of the eighteenth century new husbandry link neatly with an account of modern farming in East Anglia, there is no link between, say, the development of the jury system and the physical nature of rain clouds—to take topics that can easily be justified in a school but which clearly belong to disparate disciplines. Such problems of syllabus construction have always hampered moves towards integration. The extent to which these were fundamental problems can be seen by examining social studies syllabuses of the time. It is frequently possible, given a number of school syllabuses, to say whether the teacher responsible was a geographer or an historian by looking for the dominance of one or the other of the two disciplines.

This problem was aggravated by the lack of text books that a teacher could use for guidance. In the period of 'austerity' after the war all things were scarce including books and the money to buy them.

Social studies was rather more a secondary than a primary school experiment. It fitted the schools of the time as the new secondary modern schools were seeking to break away from the old image of the pre-1944 Act senior schools. Social studies was also seen as a possible part of the answer to the problems posed by the raising of the minimum school leaving age from fourteen to fifteen years. Despite this weighting towards secondary education, social studies was also introduced into primary schools, where it remained rather more firmly. Indeed some primary schools still follow social studies schemes.

The next movement towards integration to affect geography not only had its origins within the primary school but was almost entirely confined to such schools. This was the 'topic' approach. Topic evolved from an earlier idea, the 'centre of interest' whereby all the work of a class or even a school revolved round one theme for a period of a week or more. This complete abolition of the timetable was modified in the topic method. As this method was originally set forward, a topic was selected from the interests of a class. Thus 'dinners' or 'transport' or 'how things move' might be chosen. This was then studied from all aspects, ignoring subject boundaries where they hindered the work. Teachers trained in the topic approach were encouraged to bring in as many of the subjects listed on the timetable as possible and to make as many links as possible. Thus if the topic was dinners children were encouraged to study what people ate in the past (history), and where foods come from (geography). They drew pictures linked with the topic (art) and wrote about dinners (English). At times this was carried to ridiculous lengths. It is not an exaggeration to say that there were student teachers, in training in the early '60s when interest in this technique was at its height, who, given dinners as a topic, scoured libraries to find poems and pieces of music linked with the title and even went to the length of including an account of the miracle of the loaves and fishes.

Almost from its inception, the topic approach was closely identified with two other groups of educational ideas. First was the move away from the situation where every step undertaken was directly authorised and directed by the teacher. Following this concept of teaching the teacher might adopt a consultative, guiding and stimulating role rather than a purely didactic one. A second group of educational ideas were those particularly associated with psychological development. Basic to this group of ideas is the conclusion that most children only learn efficiently from concrete situations and so stress must be placed on activities and experiences.

The close identification of the topic approach with what are frequently called 'modern methods' is possibly confusing. The two are separate. It is possible to follow a topic approach yet use far too authoritarian a teaching technique: similarly it is very possible for children to follow a traditional scheme of geographical study that nevertheless involves a large measure of activity, experience and discovery.

Yet it is the case that some schools, through a misunderstanding of these ideas, divide the day into the formal traditional periods and the topic periods when activities are carried on.

The topic approach form of integration is very widely used and demonstrably many schools have achieved very real success by following it. Unfortunately as an approach it embodies certain difficulties. Thus it is extremely difficult to select a theme that has, quite genuinely, arisen from the interest of a class. In many cases the topic is imposed. This could be, perhaps, of no great moment for enthusiasm is infectious and children will develop interests in something that is clearly of great interest to a well-liked teacher. Still, when topics are imposed there is the risk that the choice will not be entirely suitable. 'Water' or 'travel', to quote two examples, are far too wide. A study of water, unless limited by the teacher, could justifiably involve the study of rain clouds, Egyptian irrigation, the English Channel and the hot water system of the school. These things are just as divorced from each other in the minds of children as is the material of traditional subjects. Similarly many topics that are imposed often deal with such things as 'tea' or 'the Tudors'—either of which could be handled fully and satisfactorily under a tradional form of syllabus that included both geography and history. Indeed 'topic approaches' can degenerate into a blend of geography and history, with art demoted to a purely subsidiary role as means of illustrating the children's folders. It is in this blending of geography and history that geography frequently loses much of its educational value. Some aspects of geography link logically and usefully with history, but this is seldom the case with the scientific and mathematical aspects of the subject. Thus geography is robbed of the value that lies in its character as deriving material from both the sciences and the humanities.

In extreme cases topic work can indeed achieve the opposite of what is intended. This can be seen in those schools where fixed periods have been set aside for topic work. In some classes topic work has been allowed to become little more than a prolonged exercise in the use of reference books, with schools yielding to parental demands for homework by 'encouraging' children to spend time at home laboriously copying out slabs of text following a plan dictated by the teacher. Under these circumstances it is indicative that children talk of topic lessons in exactly the same way as they speak of arithmetic lessons or spelling lessons.

More recently integration in primary schools has taken a new form: that usually referred to as 'environmental studies'. The choice of the term is significant. Just as social studies reflected a climate of opinion in the '50s, so environment—along with the allied ideas embodied in the words 'pollution 'and 'conservation'— reflect widely-held interests that grew up in the late '60s.

Environmental studies has affected both primary and secondary schools, although in the latter its development has been more complex involving team teaching and complex schemes of interdisciplinary studies. In primary schools the much simpler school organisation on a one teacher—one class basis has resulted in a newer pattern of integration in which geography, history and science hold key places.

As a pattern of work environmental studies has certain advantages over earlier forms of integration. Above all circumstances have changed. An individual teacher or a small group of teachers making up a school staff are far less isolated professionally than was the case even only a few years ago. The work of the Schools Council for the Curriculum and Examinations must be mentioned here. This council was set up in 1964 to facilitate the exchange of ideas and to enlist the help of teachers in curriculum changes, thus attempting to remedy the situation that had existed whereby, throughout this entire century, any changes in the curriculum of schools have been done by the almost entirely uncoordinated efforts of individuals or small groups. A particular contribution of the Schools Council has been in the field of primary science, in conjuction with the Nuffield primary science project. This interest in primary science has enabled the new field of environmental studies to be more broadly based, and it has enabled the scientific aspects of primary geography to be included more naturally than in any previous attempts at integration.

A second factor working to the advantage of environmental studies has been the setting up of teachers' centres. These centres, urged by the Schools Council and largely springing from teachers' own needs and initiatives, but established and supported by L.E.A.s and university institutes of education, have also helped to break down the professional isolation of teachers. The exchange of ideas at teachers' centres has meant that environmental studies has been discussed and its possibilities explored more fully than was the case with previous schemes of combined studies.

The most serious objection to environmental studies comes, as in other forms of integration, in that formulating a syllabus is very difficult. Certainly, taken as a study with a single central theme it offers far more chance for a teacher to build up a balanced scheme than did the topic approach with its somewhat haphazard selection of things to be studied. Nevertheless great difficulties arise in attempting to draw up a syllabus except when the syllabus is couched in very general terms of concepts to be introduced. The query has been raised as to whether too much importance has been given to graded syllabuses in the past. It is argued that while there is a vital need for a graded, or even a programmed, scheme in the teaching of reading, there is less need for such a detailed plan in geography. Certainly the two studies differ. In the teaching of reading it would appear logical to analyse the words that children meet, to select the most useful, and to rearrange these words in order of reading difficulty. Geography has no such clear cut order. Even in the case of history, the subject with which geography has been most usually integrated, a chronological order automatically suggests itself. There is nothing comparable in geography: indeed it is from this lack of an obvious order that most problems of syllabus construction spring. Only in the case of map work can a clear grading in terms of order of difficulty be achieved.

However the idea of a syllabus for geography expressed generally in terms of concepts is hardly likely to aid an inexperienced teacher or a teacher who has little specialised knowledge of geography in planning work for a class.

Since geography is intimately involved in nearly every case of integration in schools for younger children it is desirable to evaluate its place. Any such evaluation is difficult, except in general terms, in view of the wide diversity of interpretation given to the word integration. Within these limitations however it can be said that there is little reason to refute the argument that a rigid division of the curriculum into subjects tends to interrupt children's trains of thought and hinders them from realising the common elements in problem solving. It is equally difficult to refute the argument that if geography is taught with a full appreciation of what modern geography entails then undeniable educational benefit accrues to it. Stress is laid on a modern view of geography. There is little to be said in favour of a view of geography that allows it to be little more than topographical description to give background detail to history or anthropological description as in the case of the Eskimoes (who still appear in at least one school's brand-new scheme of integrated environmental studies as an example of a harsh environment).

Unhappily evaluating some schemes of integration involves setting the advantages of avoiding subject barriers against the loss of some of the educational value of geography. Thus there is some evidence from children admitted to secondary schools that standards of geographical knowledge are falling. This is probably inevitable when a carefully structured syllabus is discarded. However it is virtually impossible to set this against a fuller understanding of concepts and draw up a profit and loss account. Even a carefully controlled group experiment is likely to be misleading since a really enthusiastic teacher often achieves results despite flaws in the approach that is used, while a teacher who feels that an idea has been imposed by educational theorists is unlikely to achieve really good results despite the fact that the idea may be excellent.

It would follow that any new scheme of integration should be examined carefully by every teacher to see that the 'man and land' causal inter-relationship of geography is preserved, that geography is used, as it can be so effectively, to link the humanities with the sciences, and that the techniques of geography, including field studies, observation and experiment, recording in all its forms as well as its comparative techniques are included. Interpreted fully and broadly, geography is a key factor in any scheme of integration with younger children, and thus assumes a new importance.